Leviticus on the Butcher's Block

"With both the hands-on insights and the practical humor of a professional butcher, Bray brings sacrifice to life, dissecting relevant paragraphs of the biblical narrative while scrutinizing nuances of its original Hebrew text. The result is an ingenious investigation of rituals and practices that once formed the core of Jewish temple worship for a millennium and later became an important source of metaphors for the Christian church."

—CHRISTIAN A. EBERHART, author of *The Sacrifice of Jesus: Understanding Atonement Biblically*

"For centuries, theologians and pastors have gone on and on about the meaning of Old Testament sacrifices. Yet they were mostly ignorant of the practical realities of these rituals—realities in which the butchers of the world are immersed day after day. The rituals of sacrifice cannot be understood apart from the practicalities of slaughtering animals and handling meat and blood, since the meaning of any ritual is in the experience of it. Phil Bray has done us a great service by bridging this gap, giving us insight into how someone familiar with slaughter, meat, and blood (as were the priests and worshipers of the Bible) would have experienced and understood these rituals."

—JEREMY DAVIS, author of *Welcoming Gifts: Sacrifice in the Bible and Christian Life*

"This is a book to savor. Indeed, it may make you hungry for a rib eye! But Bray's achievement is to make Leviticus, possibly the most baffling book in the Old Testament, appetizing. *Leviticus on the Butcher's Block* is that rare beast: well-researched, insightful, and a delight to read."

—MICHAEL P. JENSEN, author of *Subjects and Citizens: The Politics of the Gospel*

"Too many Christians in industrialized societies read about sacrifice from a sanitized distance. Phil Bray combines his professional experience as a butcher with a deep love of scripture to draw a portrait of biblical sacrifice that practically leaps off the page. The result is accessible and vivid but also grounded in responsible scholarship. Readers who feel lost in the early chapters of Leviticus will find in this book a beautiful guide to the way God's love was expressed through these specific cultural practices."

—Abby Kaplan, author of *Misreading Ritual: Sacrifice and Purity for the Modern-Day Gentile*

"Using his experience as a butcher, Phil Bray has provided a much needed and approachable bridge between the ancient world of the Torah and that of the modern Christian. This book explains the biblical and cultural significance behind many key elements found in Leviticus's ritual texts and provides needed correctives to common assumptions along the way. If you are seeking a resource to quickly help you understand the often confusing world of Leviticus, you will find this book a great help to your biblical studies and an enjoyable read."

—Caleb S. Lewis, author of *Through the Waters: A Biblical Theology of the Book of Genesis*

"I felt deeply engaged and a bit hungry as soon as I started reading Phil's work. Phil helped me read Leviticus by infusing the biblical text with the smells of herbs and barbeque, the sounds of sharpening knives and cutting meat, and the physical work of being a butcher. He's made a lasting impression on the way I read Leviticus! More importantly, Phil focuses on how God was not bloodthirsty, but was cleansing and restoring his people, and inviting them to look ahead to Christ's work of cleansing and restoring humanity on the deepest level."

—Mako A. Nagasawa, author of *Christmas with Irenaeus*

"*Leviticus on the Butcher's Block* offers an entryway into the Levitical sacrifices from the perspective of a real butcher. This guide for laypeople offers insights into the real world of Leviticus and what it meant to offer animal sacrifices in an ancient agrarian world. With stories from life behind the knife, Bray brings the reality of sacrifice into the modern world. With accessible language, stories, and theological insights, *Leviticus on the Butcher's Block* makes a compelling case for why this ancient biblical book is so important for Christians today."

—Mark Scarlata, senior lecturer in Old Testament, St Mellitus College, London

"This book is sure to nourish our minds with the juicy layers of the book of Leviticus. Not only will it help us form biblical imaginations, but we might just fall in love with parts of Scripture that we tend to cut out and leave high and dry in our Bible study. Understanding the language, imagery, and purpose of the core of the Torah will help us better see the Messiah and live into our purposes in the church today. Welcome to the table of biblical studies; once you develop a taste for Leviticus, you will never read Scripture the same way again."

—CAREY GRIFFEL, host, *Genesis Marks the Spot* podcast

"For many Christian people living in the West 'sacrifice' is an abstract concept that exists only in the world of ideas. In this unique book, Bray marshals his experience as a butcher to open new perspectives on the reality. The copious mentions of blood, fat, and meat throughout Leviticus are not merely gratuitous or barbaric. Instead, they construct and convey rich theological truths about YHWH, his people, and the world. Be prepared to hear Leviticus like you never have before!"

—G. GEOFFREY HARPER, lecturer in Old Testament,
Sydney Missionary and Bible College

"Leviticus is often seen as the gristle of the Old Testament, but in *Leviticus on the Butcher's Block* Bray transforms this tough text into a theological feast. With the precision of a master butcher and the pastoral heart of a shepherd, Bray cuts through the complexities of sacrifice to reveal its rich, gospel-centered flavor, pointing us to the Lamb who takes away sin. Accessible, witty, and profoundly Christ-centered, this book invites readers to savor God's holiness, grace, and the ultimate sacrifice fulfilled in Jesus. Leviticus has never tasted so rich—or satisfying."

—MATT REDMOND, author of *The Forgetful Prince*

Leviticus on the Butcher's Block

Making Head or Tail of the Bible's Toughest Book

↢

PHIL BRAY

Foreword by MAX BOTNER

RESOURCE *Publications* · Eugene, Oregon

LEVITICUS ON THE BUTCHER'S BLOCK
Making Head or Tail of the Bible's Toughest Book

Resource Publications
An Imprint of Wipf and Stock Publishers
199 W. 8th Ave., Suite 3
Eugene, OR 97401

www.wipfandstock.com

PAPERBACK ISBN: 979-8-3852-4033-3
HARDCOVER ISBN: 979-8-3852-4034-0
EBOOK ISBN: 979-8-3852-4035-7

All illustrations in this book were drawn by Kiralee Bray.
And for that, Kiralee, my wife, my love: gratitude.

Contents

Foreword

LEVITICUS HAS LONG BEEN on the chopping block of Christian theology—little more than a select object lesson in how the creator of the universe requires his pound of flesh. Yet in our haste to skip over this book, grateful (if we're being honest) that its monotonous, textualized rituals no longer apply to us, we miss its bold articulation of the gospel: the triune God so desires to dwell with us that he will do whatever it takes to accommodate himself to our weaknesses (so ultimately to transform us). This is the logic of the incarnation.

Why haven't we heard this message? The primary reason is that scholarship on Leviticus tends to be highly esoteric. It takes years of study just to get a handle on the various discourses and insights that have emerged over the last several decades (since the seminal work of Jacob Milgrom). Few have an interest in doing so, and still fewer have the capacity to translate the fruit of such technical scholarship into popular Christian teaching.

Enter Phil Bray: a butcher who loves Leviticus—just the sort of rare cut for whom we've been waiting!

Bray expertly carves up the complex world of Leviticus into tantalizing slices that are sure to leave readers wanting more.

- "Biblical sacrifice [isn't about loss or death but] sharing good things with the Creator."

- "A sacrifice is an invitation to a meal. But a meal with Yahweh isn't as much about *what* you are eating, as *who* you are eating with."

- "Leviticus is the book that shows the way God plans to live in the midst of his people."

- "Yahweh's invitation to come close incorporates a whole body experience."

- "Some . . . want to see sacrifice as a payment required by God, turning it into a transaction. But this severely misrepresents God's character."

- "An offering [at least, as some of the most prominent Jewish theorists understood it] was [about] the state of the offerer's heart."

These are just some of the many insights that you will encounter in the pages that follow.

Yet Bray goes beyond merely translating insights from Leviticus. He also does the important and necessary work of theologizing from Leviticus in light of the Christ event. "Heaven has infected every part of creation," Bray reminds us, even as "Jesus came into contact with every part of human existence, in his birth, life, death, and resurrection." Thus Leviticus points ahead to the God-man in whose life we participate at the sacrificial meal to which he invites all of humanity.

I can't tell you how excited I am to see this book in the world. Leviticus belongs not on the chopping block but on the butcher's block!

Max Botner, PhD
Jessup University

Foretaste:
From Butchering to Leviticus

My CAREER AS A butcher began accidentally. I was at home playing Zak McKracken on my Commodore 64, still in my school uniform, when the phone rang. "G'day, it's Gary the butcher. Do you still want a job?"

I'd visited all my local shops asking for work, but Gary was the only one who came through with the goods. I'd clean the floors, scrub the benches, scrape the band saw, even wash Gary's panel van. I was a quiet kid, happiest with my head in a book, and becoming a qualified butcher was not at all on my agenda. My real passion was writing, and I wanted to be an author. I dreamt of working as a journalist, and writing a trilogy of fantasy novels (about a colony of sentient toadstools who live deep beneath the Mountain of Drab their ancient ruler known as the Elder Shroom whose life spores sustain the entire Realm of Fungia so long as the Elder Shroom maintains his existence in utter darkness and silence but one day the Elder Shroom's serenity is disturbed when evil fireflies infiltrate his cave infecting the darkness with light and shattering the Elder Shroom's solace with their constant chatter causing the balanced biome of the Realm of Fungia to descend into chaos until a grumpy giant named Parsley is awakened from his hundred year slumber and leaves his home to find the reclusive badger wizard who is an expert in fungal magic and together the unlikely pair embark on a quest to unearth the Spore of Destiny and restore equanimity to the Realm of Fungia—will they succeed or will the evil forces of light prevail . . .)

But when it came time to finish school and think about a university, the Bible got in the way. The Christian school I attended had a unique knack for teaching the Bible in such a way that it became indistinguishable from any of my other textbooks. After several years of obligatory Bible study, I guess I knew the Bible pretty well, but I didn't know the Author. I was a foie gras goose getting fat on facts from a book, but I had no love for the hand that was feeding me. As I dreamed about finishing school, and designing a pointy hat for my badger wizard, the school informed me that biblical studies was a compulsory subject, but it would not count towards my final exams. I was faced with a decision: stay at school and study the Bible under duress, or drop out and get a job.

The threat of banal Bible study made the decision for me and I quit school, abandoning my dream of becoming a famous fantasy writer. Somewhat unimaginatively I applied for a job as an apprentice butcher, and . . . I got the job. Ironically, it was the Bible that made me become a butcher, but through a strange turn of events, it would be meat that brought me back to writing—writing about the Bible no less.

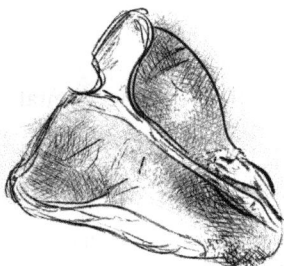

I admit there are few things stranger than loving Leviticus, and I suspect butchers who love Leviticus are even more rare. However, over time I developed a passion for ancient sacrifice, atonement, and Leviticus, so that today I could happily talk about Leviticus until the cows come home. All I will say for now is that being a butcher provides a surprising insight into the inner workings of the sacrificial process. And understanding ancient sacrifice helps demystify what Paul might mean by a *living* sacrifice.

You might have been exposed to a sliced meat delicacy consisting of various unknown ingredients, one of which is allegedly processed pork. In Australia we call it devon, but in other parts of the world it's baloney. When I was a kid and Mum took us shopping, the local butcher would give me and my brother a sneaky slice of devon as an enticement. So here I am, your local butcher from Sydney Australia, attempting to whet your appetite for the book of Leviticus. Consider this book your slice of devon, a tantalising taste, that I hope will be the beginnings of an insatiable appetite for Leviticus.

Leviticus begins by introducing the burnt offering, which is a good place to start as it contains all the elements of a Hebrew sacrifice. You'll notice that the chapters for this book were inspired by the words in bold (plus there's a free bonus chapter).

> If his offering is a **burnt offering** from the herd, he is to bring an **unblemished** male. He will **bring it to the entrance** to the tent of meeting so that he may be accepted by the LORD. He is to lay his **hand on the head** of the burnt offering so it can be accepted on his behalf to make **atonement** for him. He is to **slaughter** the bull before the LORD; Aaron's sons the priests are to present the **blood** and splatter it on all sides of the altar that is at the entrance to the tent of meeting. Then he is to skin the burnt offering and **cut it into pieces**. The sons of Aaron the priest will prepare a fire on the altar and arrange wood on the fire. Aaron's sons the priests are to arrange the pieces, the head, and the **fat** on top of the burning wood on the altar. The offerer is to wash its entrails and legs with water. Then the priest will burn all of it on the altar as a burnt offering, a **food offering**, a **pleasing aroma** to the LORD. (Lev 1:3–9 CSB)

First Cut: Where Does the Burnt Offering Go?

WHAT'S THE BEST MEAT to roast for a family of five? Well, dear customer, my best advice to you is that whatever roasting meat you put in the oven will come out weighing 25 percent less. Where does the 25 percent go? It goes up in smoke. Well, technically, the 25 percent is mostly moisture loss, but if you kept cooking, your family roast would eventually shrivel and disappear up in smoke. With the burnt offering however, the whole lot, not just 25 percent, was sent up in smoke to God.

The burnt offering is described in chapter 1 of Leviticus, but the Hebrew word doesn't actually mean *burnt*. It is, however, related to what happens when something burns. The Hebrew word literally means *going up*, or *ascend*. Ezekiel uses this word to describe "steps going up" (Ezek 40:26). When something burns it is turned into smoke that rises up into the heavens. In ancient imagination God was "up there" in the heavens, and the dead went "down there" under the ground. The term *offer up* is all bound up in this idea of going upwards. So the burnt offering could be called a *going up offering* or an *offering of ascent*. This is a good first step to understanding what a sacrifice was for: sending something upwards to God. The burnt offering is literally *turned into smoke* (Lev 1:13) and sent upwards to Yahweh.

One of the confusions I've encountered is how we as modern people hear the phrase *giving up*, or even the word *sacrifice*. In

2001 a mean spirited little man made a moderately stirring speech. "Some of you may die, but it's a sacrifice I am willing to make."[1]

If you were to open your modern English dictionary, you would find sandwiched between *sacred* and *sacrilege* the word *sacrifice*, with a definition something like: "the act of giving up something that you want to keep."[2] That's pretty much what sacrifice had always meant to my modern mind: giving something up, or denying myself something good. But biblical sacrifice is not giving something up like giving up meat for Lent, or giving up coffee for a month; it's not giving up to go without, rather the giving is directional. Biblical sacrifice is more *giving upwards*.

There are five offerings described in the first few chapters of Leviticus: the burnt offering (Lev 1, 6:8–13), the grain offering (Lev 2, 6:14–23), the peace offering (Lev 3, 7:11–36), the sin offering (Lev 4:1—5:13, 6:24–30), and the guilt offering (Lev 5:14—6:7, 7:1–7). The burnt offering is unique from all other offerings because the *entire* offering is given upwards to God—God gets all of it. It actually gets translated as the "whole burnt offering" in the Septuagint, the ancient Greek translation of the Old Testament. With all other offerings, the priests get some, and with the peace offering, after the priest takes his portion, the rest is taken back home to the offerer's family. But the burnt offering belongs entirely to Yahweh.

Australia's highest priced bull, an Angus named Texas Thunderstruck, sold in northern New South Wales for three hundred sixty thousand dollars (you could buy a house in Alice Springs with that money). Today, as in ancient Israel, a bull is an expensive

1. Adamson and Jenson, *Shrek*. Spoken by Lord Farquaad.
2. *Britannica Dictionary*, "Sacrifice."

asset. To give a whole bull to God meant you were giving something valuable, something precious and truly meaningful. That's the thing about the burnt offering—it's about giving your very best to God. Not scrounging around in the bottom of the fridge for some floppy carrots, or regifting that shirt you didn't really like—it's selecting the best that you have, and offering it entirely up to God.

You may notice a hole in my analogy, however; regifting a shirt may seem in poor taste, but, if you think about it, who gave the bull to Israel in the first place? If you want to be pedantic, giving a bull to Yahweh could be seen as a regifted animal. Besides, what could anyone give God that he doesn't already have?

> I do not rebuke you for your sacrifices
> or for your burnt offerings,
> which are continually before me.
> I will not take a bull from your household
> or male goats from your pens,
> for every animal of the forest is mine,
> the cattle on a thousand hills.
> I know every bird of the mountains,
> and the creatures of the field are mine. (Ps 50:8–11 CSB)

Have you ever had cake shoved into your mouth by a two-year-old? My daughter experienced cake in a special way: legs kicking, arms flapping, bouncing in her chair, she would extend a fistful of cake towards me. I gave her the cake, but her innocent joyful reaction was to share it with me. What I'm trying to say is this: God gave Israel cake, and his desire was to share in their abundant joy. Biblical sacrifice is not defined by sadness or a sense of deprivation. Biblical sacrifice is about sharing good things with the Creator.

My wife loves receiving gifts, and one thing I know: nothing says *I love you* like socks and underpants. Nothing says *I value you* like a gift voucher . . . is something I would never ever say. Because they are not special gifts. They're useful. They may be practical. But they lack panache. If I'm trying to demonstrate my love and devotion, something overly gratuitous may be more suitable, like saving up to buy a diamond ring or splashing out on a big bunch of flowers. And so when an ancient Israelite wanted to show their devotion and gratitude to Yahweh they would have thought Texas Thunderstruck, not socks and underpants.

Leviticus, though, is not the first time a burnt offering has shown up in the Bible. Noah presented a burnt offering after being kept safe through the flood (Gen 8:20), hundreds of years before Leviticus was ever written down. Nor were burnt offerings unique to Israel. In fact, it was likely the norm for most cultures and people in the ancient world. Have a read of Homer's *The Iliad* (eighth century BC), and you'll find they offered sacrifices more often than they had hot dinners. Even as early as Gen 4, Cain and Abel brought "offerings to Yahweh." Had God asked for these offerings? Or has there always been some innate desire within humans to give a gift to God? Either way, Leviticus is where God gives guidelines to his people around what kinds of gifts he likes to receive, while not so subtly showing them that some of their neighbours' rituals are emphatically *not* okay, like offering human sacrifice, eating blood, or killing the animal on the altar.

But what exactly were they offering up? Did Yahweh need an animal? Why did he desire a dead one?

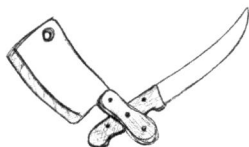

You shall offer a male lamb one year old without blemish for a burnt offering to Yahweh. Its grain offering shall then be two-tenths of an ephah of fine flour mixed with oil, an offering by fire to Yahweh for a soothing aroma, with its drink offering, a fourth of a hin of wine. (Lev 23:12–13)

A big splash of wine, poured over the burnt offering was not uncommon. And the grain offering (Lev 2) was often combined with the burnt offering, presented together to Yahweh as a pleasing aroma. Grain offerings could include cakes of fine flour, frankincense, wafers spread with oil, and grain cooked in a pan.

The whole burnt offering is placed on the flames and sent upwards in smoke. A priest watches the smoke ascending up to heaven. He closes his eyes, takes a long, deep breath. Heady frankincense fills his nostrils. The roasting pieces spit and crackle on the flames. Sizzling oil, popping grain, wine, wafting and swirling up to Yahweh as a pleasing aroma.

Frankly, it sounds delicious, and it's beginning to sound a lot like food, and less like a dead animal. There's no doubt it was a pleasing aroma, but what exactly was being placed on the altar? Was Yahweh hungry?

Second Slice: Why Is the Offering Cut into Pieces?

He will cut the animal into pieces with its head and its fat,
and the priest will arrange them on top of the burning wood on the altar.
(Lev 1:12 CSB)

WAIT, WHAT!? WHY HAVE I been banging on about the *whole* burnt offering only to discover it's cut into pieces?

As a butcher, I cut up lamb cutlets and arrange them on a tray. I try to keep them as uniform as possible so they cook evenly, and so they've got a nice bit of bone to hold as you tear off the meat with your teeth. But when a priest cut up a lamb and arranged it on the altar, what was he doing? Shortly, we will sink our teeth into what *was* being placed on top of the altar, but first I want to notice what was *not* placed on God's altar.

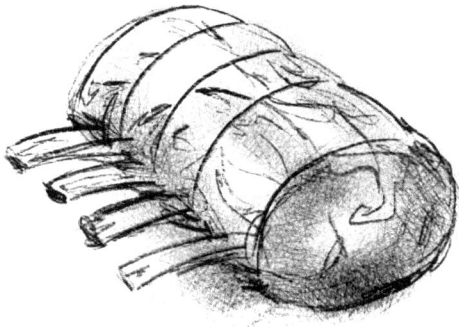

There are perfectly good Hebrew words for *corpse* and *carcass*. One is the word used by God to explain to the Israelites what will become of them since they did not want to enter the promised land: "your corpses will fall in this wilderness" (Num 14:32 CSB). *Corpses* and *carcasses* do occur in Leviticus, particularly in chapter 11, where we are told about animal carcasses, mostly to *avoid* them, because they are unclean and should not be touched: "anyone who touches its carcass will be unclean till evening" (Lev 11:39 NIV).

As I searched through Leviticus for animal corpses and dead carcasses, I made a discovery that stopped me dead in my tracks.

> He shall slaughter the *bull* before the LORD; and Aaron's sons the priests shall offer up the blood and sprinkle the blood around on the altar that is at the doorway of the tent of meeting. He shall then skin the *burnt offering* and cut it into its pieces. (Lev 1:5–6 NASB, emphasis added)

The words *carcass* and *corpse* are never used to refer to what goes on God's altar. An animal carcass is never given to God and a corpse is never placed on his altar. In fact, an *animal* is never placed on God's altar. Consistently throughout Leviticus, after an animal is killed the language fundamentally changes; it has ceased to be an *animal* and has now become an *offering*.

We'll explore the slaughter of the animal in a later chapter, but for now I want to dissect what exactly *was* being placed on the altar. You may have seen pictures of a whole dead lamb on the altar. This never happened. A gruesome bloody dead animal has no place on God's altar. We know that whatever was placed on Yahweh's altar was a gift, a gift given upwards to God. This in itself should be a dead giveaway, because who would want to be given a corpse? But let me offer a butcher's perspective. When I walk into the cool room, I do not see dead animals hanging up. I have never ordered a dead pig or a cow carcass. No, what I see hanging in my cool room is pork and bodies of beef. So what *is* being placed on God's altar? Whatever it is has been carefully skinned, washed, divided into portions, and all the pieces have been carefully arranged on top of the wood on the fire (Lev 1:6–9).

When I order a whole body of beef it arrives in four parts: two forequarters and two hindquarters. It has been skinned, washed, and the head and tail have already been removed as have all the internal organs. A sacrificial offering was also cut up into pieces, but I suspect the portions were smaller than four quarters, and while we don't know how small the portion sizes were, I doubt they were cutting cutlets or slicing steaks.

Something that excites me as a butcher, but something I was not at all expecting, is the amount of space given to the instructions around preparing the pieces. The actual slaughter of the animal was done by the person bringing the offering, but the priests were tasked with the preparation, and so it seems a big part of a priest's time was spent butchering! And so, of course, a big part of Leviticus is dedicated to describing this butchering process. A surprisingly big part.

Let's take a peep over the countertop, and see what we might find on the priests' butchers block.

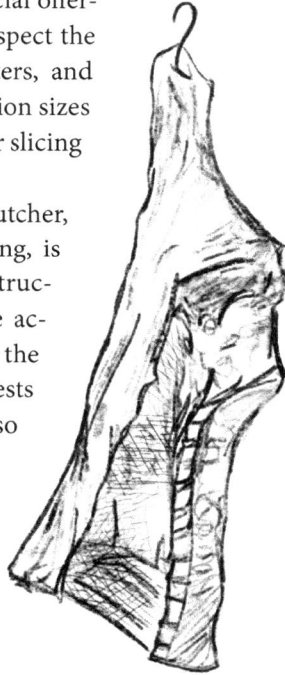

> . . . a side room, where the meat for sacrifices was washed. . . . There were eight tables in all—four inside and four outside—where the sacrifices were cut up and prepared. There were also four tables of finished stone for preparation of the burnt offerings. . . . On these tables were placed the butchering knives and other implements for slaughtering the sacrificial animals. There were hooks, each 3 inches long, fastened to the foyer walls. The sacrificial meat was laid on the tables. (Ezek 40:38–43 NLT)

This image comes significantly later than Leviticus, but the New Living Translation mentions butchering knives which is a bit fun. Also, in Ezekiel's vision of this new temple, instead of wooden butchering blocks there are stone tables for cutting up and preparing the pieces, which makes me cringe thinking about how cutting on stone would damage my knives!

SKIN

Back in Leviticus—an initial important step in the process is the skinning. At a modern day abattoir, after the slaughter, the animal is hung up, a few precise cuts are made, and then a hydraulic de-hiding machine peels the entire skin off in one go. The Hebrews hadn't invented hydraulic pistons yet so they had to use a knife.

> The priest who brings near any man's burnt offering, that priest shall have for himself the skin of the burnt offering. (Lev 7:8)

The Levites were not allotted land like the other Israelite tribes, and so the priests relied on portions from the Israelite offerings. Part of the priests' portion was these skins, whether for leather, clothing, bedding, or tents.

HEAD

I don't know about elsewhere in the world, but in Sydney we never receive bodies of beef with the head. Lambs come with the head removed, and bodies of pork mostly arrive headless. When I was an apprentice, on rare occasions we would receive a pork body with the head still attached. Apparently all pork used to come with the head, but over the years as they resurfaced and resealed the abattoir floors the floor got higher. As they hung upside down, the head was now too close to the ground and there was a risk of picking up contamination from the floor. So, rather than lowering the floor height, they just removed the heads.

> He is to lay his hand on the head of the burnt offering. . . .
> The priests are to arrange the pieces, the head, and the fat
> on top of the burning wood on the altar. (Lev 1:4, 8 CSB)

I find it interesting that the head is specifically placed alongside the portions on the altar and given to God. I wonder, too, what ramifications this may have, because I notice the offerer placed a hand on the head before it was slaughtered, then that head ends up as part of the pleasing aroma ascending to God. More on that in a later chapter . . .

GUTS AND LEGS

He is to wash the entrails and legs with water. The priest will then present all of it and burn it on the altar. (Lev 1:13 CSB)

The entrails and legs are washed, then placed on the fire with the rest of the burnt offering. Because God got the whole lot. I've never seen a cow use a toilet, so presumably as they walked around in the field, they got dirty feet. Similarly, washing the entrails ensures the offering is kept safe from any unclean contaminants.

LIVERS, KIDNEYS, AND FAT

And from the sacrifice of peace offerings he shall bring near as an offering by fire to Yahweh its fat, the entire fat tail which he shall remove close to the backbone, and the fat that covers the entrails and all the fat that is on the entrails, and the two kidneys with the fat that is on them, which is on the loins, and the lobe of the liver, which he shall remove with the kidneys. (Lev 3:9–10)

God got *all* of the burnt offering, but now, as we read about the peace offering, we are told that Yahweh gets specific parts only. When I have a whole lamb sitting on my butcher's block and I look inside, all down the centre along the backbone there is a thick layer of fat. This encases the kidneys and protects the liver and internal organs. Leviticus tells us that these bits all belong to Yahweh: the kidneys, a portion of the liver, and all the fat that surrounds them. These were considered the *best bits* and were reserved for Yahweh alone, and, whether you like offal or not, we're going to talk at length about livers, kidneys, and fat in a later chapter.

BREASTS AND THIGHS

The breast shall belong to Aaron and his sons. And you shall give the right thigh to the priest as a contribution from the sacrifices of your peace offerings. (Lev 7:31–32)

Continuing with more sacrificial contributions, the right thigh and the breast were both part of the priestly quota. The portions that these fortunate priests received were so desirable that a later Jewish rabbi and poet fancies himself to be a *lucky priest*, as he writes erotically about a woman's breasts and thighs.[1] Later in chapter 10 it is reiterated that the breast and the thigh are for the priests and their family, "because these portions have been assigned to you and your children from the Israelites' fellowship sacrifices" (Lev 10:14 CSB).

The priestly butchers have been hard at work breaking up a burnt offering into its portions: the breast and the thigh, the head, the kidneys, the fat, a part of the liver, washed entrails, all placed on Yahweh's altar—it was even salted! "With all your offerings you shall offer salt" (Lev 2:13 ESV).

---

1. It is a token of how keenly the concrete details of these seemingly dry cultic passages were reflected on by later generations that Moses ibn Ezra (ca. 1055–1135) should wittily invoke these body parts in an erotic poem, transposing them from animal to woman, and proclaiming that he will take his due portion as did the priests of old. The ingenious allusion registers a sound exegetical understanding that the breast and the thigh are the choice parts. Alter, *Hebrew Bible*, 392, footnote on Lev 7:34.

So what is God being given? If a dead animal is never placed on his altar, if Yahweh isn't being given a carcass, perhaps after it has been carefully divided into portions it is now considered what today we might call *meat*?

Third Portion: Is Yahweh Hungry for a Food Offering?

IF YOU LEFT LEVITICUS and hopped ahead to Hebrews, you would find it says that *both gifts and sacrifices are offered, which relate only to food and drink* (9:9–10). Sacrifices relate only to food and drink? Closer to home, Numbers mentions food for Yahweh, as does Malachi.

> You shall be careful to present to Me My offering, My food for My offerings by fire, of a soothing aroma to Me. (Num 28:2)
>
> You are presenting defiled food upon My altar. (Mal 1:7)

With these tasty morsels for context, we should not be too shocked to learn that Leviticus calls the burnt offering "a food offering, a pleasing aroma to the LORD" (Lev 1:9 CSB, also NIV, ESV). The grain offering consisted of fine flour and olive oil made into cakes, or wafers coated with oil, which were baked in an oven or cooked in a pan. As if this didn't already sound very food-like and delicious, this too is called a *food offering* (Lev 2:2–5).

Other translations might use the term *offering by fire* rather than *food offering*. The key ingredient to understand what's cooking is the phrase *pleasing aroma*. Almost every time you see the words *food offering* they appear alongside the words *pleasing aroma*. We'll sniff out the significance behind the pleasing aroma in a later chapter, but it seems Yahweh loves the smell of baked grain and roasting meat.

Simply put: what is being placed on Yahweh's altar is *food*.

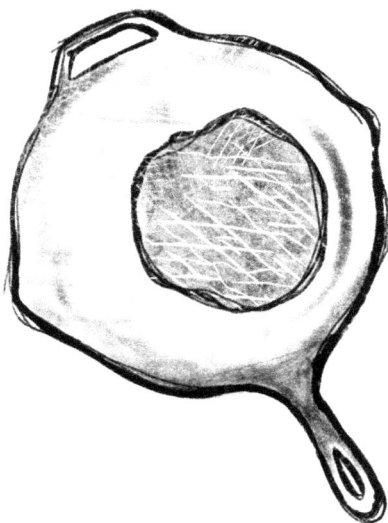

I recently heard about a Japanese tradition of using chopsticks with points at both ends. They're called *iwai-bashi*, and are used for New Year celebrations. Normally only one end—the food end—is pointed, but with these chopsticks both ends are pointed, because one end is used by the person, and the other end by the gods. This represents the gods and people eating together.

Why feed a god? Why place food on Yahweh's altar and burn it up? Was Yahweh hungry? In Ps 50 Yahweh pulls no punches when reproving his people for their lacklustre attitude towards his sacrifices. "Every beast of the forest is Mine" says Yahweh. "And everything that moves in the field is Mine. If I were hungry I would not tell you, for the world is Mine." No, Yahweh does not need to be fed. Instead, Yahweh says he would rather his people offer "a sacrifice of thanksgiving" (Ps 50:10–14, 23).

So why *was* food placed on Yahweh's altar? Hold onto that thought for a second.

Ezekiel 46 talks about kitchens and ovens in the temple where the Levites cooked their food. It says they boiled the guilt and the sin offerings, and baked the grain offerings. It seems that, by the time Ezekiel is writing, it had become such a prominent part of the temple worship practices that whole kitchens were constructed. "These are the kitchens where those who minister at the temple will cook the people's sacrifices" (Ezek 46:24 CSB).

Last chapter we learned the priests got the skins from the offerings, from which they made bedding and clothing. They received the breasts and the thighs, too, and now we know what they did with these: they ate them! Leviticus proceeds to lay out specific instructions around who is to benefit from these culinary gifts.

> Every grain offering that is baked in the oven and everything prepared in a pan or on a griddle shall belong to the priest who brings it near. (Lev 7:9)

The priests' food had to be eaten in a *ceremonially clean place*, and the sin offering is specifically said to be *most holy*. "The sin offering is most holy . . . the priest who offers it as a sin offering will eat it. It is to be eaten in a holy place" (Lev 6:25–26 CSB).[1] Access to holy food, however, came with certain conditions. Leviticus 22 presents a list of reasons why a priest could *not* eat from the holy gifts. Anyone with a skin disease, anyone who had come in contact with a corpse, anyone who had touched an unclean animal, or who had had sex, all these things rendered a priest unclean and unable to eat holy food.

> A person who touches any such thing shall be unclean until evening and shall not eat of the holy gifts unless he has bathed his body in water. But the sun will set, and he will be clean. And afterward he shall eat of the holy gifts, for it is his food. (Lev 22:6–7)

We will dive into ritual cleansing in the bonus chapter, for now, though, it wasn't only the priests who were able to eat the

---

1. It is evidently important that the priests eat the sin offering, yet the only reason given is that they *bear the iniquity* (*nasa avon*) of Israel (Lev 10:17). Although it is not entirely clear *how* a priest eating the sin offering *bears sin* (*nasa avon*), the priests are acting as God's representatives, and Yahweh is also said to *nasa avon*, although when Yahweh bears sin it is usually translated as *forgive iniquity* (Exod 34:1; Ps 25:8; Ps 32:5). Wait till chapter 12 for more on *nasa*.

food from the offerings. The priests' entire families were included in this welfare system. The slave of a priest, or a resident employee, and "those who are born in his house may eat of his food" (22:11). Likewise, if a priest's daughter became a widow or was divorced, "she shall eat of her father's food" (22:13).

Those priestly portions from the peace offerings were to be shared with their families too. Yahweh said to them; the breast and the thigh "you may eat in a clean place, you and your sons and your daughters with you; for they have been given as a statute for you and a statute for your sons taken out of the sacrifices of the peace offerings of the sons of Israel" (Lev 10:14).

Humans eating food makes sense. But what about food for God? When my son Asher was three, he would prepare me meals of plastic fruit, and cups of plastic tea. "That's delicious!" I would exclaim as I pretended to chew a plastic watermelon. Whether or not I was hungry did not matter. Whether or not I actually ate wasn't the point. Asher's intention wasn't to "feed me" nor was he trying to win me over; he just wanted to spend time with his dad.

As an analogy, a father and his child participating in a mock meal goes some way to describe the mindset behind a sacrifice. A sacrifice is an invitation to a meal. But a meal with Yahweh isn't as much about *what* you are eating, as *who* you are eating with. Presenting food to Yahweh was understood as sitting at Yahweh's table, and in Israel's ancient culture, sharing a table with someone was a big deal. When two parties shared a meal it signified mutual friendship, peace, and protection.

The prophet Malachi records some harsh words for a handful of priests who were showing contempt for Yahweh's table. Whether or not those priests acknowledged their iniquity, the harsh words helpfully demonstrate how Yahweh's altar and his table are intertwined.

> You are presenting defiled food upon My altar. But you say, "How have we defiled You?" In that you say, "The table of Yahweh is to be despised." . . .You are profaning it, in that you say, "The table of the Lord is defiled, and as for its fruit, its food is to be despised." (Mal 1:7, 12)

PEACE OFFERING

If you ever become as obsessed with sacrifice as me, you may understand why I almost jumped out of my skin when reading through Leviticus for the hundredth time and noticed that the word *sacrifice* doesn't show up till chapter 3. Does that mean that chapters 1 and 2, the burnt and the grain offerings, are not sacrifices? It's not until the peace offering that the word sacrifice first appears.

Unless you're reading the KJV, pretty much every time you read the word *sacrifice* in your English Bible, you are reading the Hebrew word *zebah*. A sacrifice (*zebah*) is distinct from an offering (*qorban*). To be precise, a sacrifice is an offering, but not all offerings are sacrifices. I'll try to be less cryptic: basically, in the Hebrew Bible, an offering (*qorban*) only becomes a sacrifice (*zebah*) if it is shared as a meal. To look at it another way, while an offering is a food gift for Yahweh, a sacrifice is an opportunity for the community to share that meal with Yahweh.[2]

2. Father Jeremy Davis unpacks this in his amazing book *Welcoming Gifts: Sacrifice in the Bible and Christian Life.*

The peace offering is sometimes called a communion sacrifice, or a fellowship offering, and these are good ways to communicate the meaning of this ritual. The peace offering is portioned up by the priest: God gets his bit—the best bits; then the priests get their bits—the breast and thigh; then the worshipper takes the rest back to his family and throws a party. The picture is one of communion: everyone has their portion, the priests, the people, even God, and they all celebrate a meal together. It's a fellowship offering because it was designed to be eaten together. It's a peace offering because there are many people, participating and feasting together in peace, celebrating Yahweh and the peace he has provided. This is an invitation to the community to participate in a meal with their God.

> The meat of his thanksgiving sacrifice of fellowship must be eaten on the day he offers it; he may not leave any of it until morning. (Lev 7:15 CSB)

Ancient Hebrews did not have fridges, but I don't think the rule against storing the sacrifice was to reduce the risk of salmonella. I think it's because the idea behind the peace offering is to bring the community together. The prohibition is against storing up food for yourself. Is there too much meat? Invite more people to the party! Everyone is expected to participate in the peace and fellowship that is enjoyed in union with Yahweh.

The peace offering shares many fascinating similarities with Passover. Both Passover and the peace offering contain the warning that the meat cannot be left till the following day, and both are designed to be eaten together as a communal feast. Just as the peace offering is one animal shared among the many, so the Passover lamb is one lamb shared among a whole household. Passover is in fact called a sacrifice (Exod 12:27), but *none* of it is given to God, neither is there an altar. I think it's hugely significant that as God rescues his people from Egypt he doesn't require anything from them. Passover is like a reverse burnt offering, where, instead of God receiving, God *gives* the whole gift. God invites his children to share a meal, and he is the host.

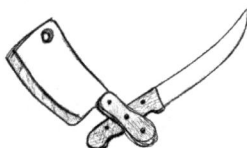

The Passover meal may be the only sacrifice in the Old Testament that wasn't shared with Yahweh. But what about today? Doesn't Yahweh still want to share a meal with his people? Of course he does.

One evening thirteen friends were gathered around a table eating the Passover meal when the host surprised them. He took bread, gave thanks, broke the bread into pieces, and said, "This is my body given for you; do this in remembrance of me" (Luke 22:19 NIV).

Jesus transformed the Passover sacrifice into the regular remembrance meal that today we call *Holy Communion*, or the *Eucharist*. And at this meal, he is the host, it is at his table we eat, he is the gift, and he is the meal. And, echoing the principles behind the peace offering, while we have been invited to join Jesus at his table, it's more than merely consuming food; eating is *participating*.

> Is not the bread that we break a participation in the body of Christ? Because there is one loaf, we, who are many, are one body, for we all share the one loaf. (1 Cor 10:16–17 NIV)

Eating the meal is a participation in and with Christ. Somehow, depending on your tradition, Christ is present in the meal. Paul's point is highlighted when he warns the Corinthians that if they sacrifice food to demons, they are participating with demons. He says, "Are not those who eat the sacrifices participants in the altar?" (1 Cor 10:18 ESV). We, however, are privileged to eat at the table of the Lord, and we who share the Lord's table are participating in Jesus himself (v. 21).

> Whoever eats My flesh and drinks My blood has eternal life, and I will raise him up at the last day. For My flesh is food indeed, and My blood is drink indeed. He who eats My flesh and drinks My blood abides in Me, and I in him. (John 6:53–58 NKJV)

Some time ago, my wife and I took a trip to Ethiopia. The group we were travelling with were coffee buyers, and so we were privileged to visit a coffee farm, and these Ethiopian coffee farmers treated us as their honoured guests. It was such a special occasion that they killed an ox for us, and, as we sat around the fire sharing strips of meat, we realised it was the first time some of the children had ever tasted beef. The lives of rural Ethiopians today are not dissimilar to those of the ancient Hebrews. We saw Ethiopian farmers tossing grain into the air and the wind blowing the chaff away, and we watched an ox tread out the grain (like in Ps 1:4 and Deut 25:4). For many Ethiopians today, eating meat is rare and costly. We know from historians and scholars that it was the same for people living in the ancient Near East; eating meat was relatively rare unless you were rich. Meat wasn't bought from a store, and it couldn't be kept in a fridge.

Although our Ethiopian friends didn't offer the ox to any gods (that I know of), it helps provide a picture of the culture we are trying to understand. In ancient cultures meat was generally only eaten when participating in a sacrificial festival. Basically, if you had meat in your mouth, you were probably at a sacrifice. There are hints of this in Leviticus where we see laws requiring all animals for food to be brought to the priest and offered at the tent (Lev 17:5). But then, once Yahweh had expanded Israel's territory, and the tent was now too far away, eating meat outside of holy space became permissible (Deut 12:20–23).

Four Quarter: Yahweh's Invitation to Bring It to the Entrance

THIS CHAPTER WILL BE an attempt to unpack the bizarre practice of bringing a food gift to a God who is not hungry. To begin to wrap our heads around this pickle we're in, have you ever wondered why Leviticus is sandwiched between Exodus and Numbers? Well, the name *Leviticus* is actually its Greek name, but the Hebrew name sets the scene much more helpfully. The Hebrew name comes from the opening words of the book: "And he called," or in Hebrew, *vayikra*. God calling out to Moses presents a problem—a problem that the book of Leviticus seeks to solve. At the end of Exodus, Moses finishes constructing the tent of meeting, precipitating Yahweh's desire to live in the midst of his people. Exodus ends with the words "the glory of Yahweh filled the tabernacle," but . . . "Moses was not able to enter" (Exod 40:34–35). Yahweh is living in the midst of his people, but no one can come and visit him.

Leviticus begins: *vayikra*, "Then Yahweh called to Moses and spoke to him from the tent of meeting" (Lev 1:1). This is a problem. Yahweh calls to Moses *from* the tent while Moses waits outside, unable to go in. However, by the time we get to the next book, something has changed. The first words of Numbers are "The LORD spoke to Moses in the tent of meeting" (Num 1:1 CS3). Moses is in! Whatever happened in Leviticus made it possible for Moses, and the people of Israel, to draw near and visit Yahweh. Leviticus is the book that shows the way God plans to live in the midst of his people, and food offerings and sacrifices are part of the recipe.

> When any man from among you brings an offering near
> to Yahweh, you shall bring your offering of animals from
> the herd or the flock. (Lev 1:2)

There are two words worth noticing: *bring* (*qorab*) and *offering* (*qorban*).[1] In Hebrew they are related, they sound similar, and they provide some nice Hebrew alliteration that doesn't come through in English. "Bring" literally means *approach*, or *draw near*, or *come close*, and this essentially is the goal of Leviticus: to enable Israel to *come close* to Yahweh, and to visit him. How is *bring near* related to the word *offering*? An *offering* (*qorban*) is in fact the thing that is *brought near*, the gift that is presented. Therefore, one way to read verse 2 could be "when anyone *brings near* their *nearness gift.*"

I'll just stick a skewer in this for now, but intriguingly the offerings come closer to Yahweh than the offerer. The animal becomes a holy offering, and ends up on Yahweh's holy table, where it ascends as smoke into heaven. In a later chapter we'll discover how once a year the *life* of an unblemished animal comes even closer, coming all the way into Yahweh's holy dwelling place, coming into contact with Yahweh's footstool, right where his presence appears.

The very physical act of drawing near and bringing a food gift demonstrates that a sacrifice is not just about ticking a box. A sacrifice is not an impassive transaction. Through the visceral ritual of sacrifice, Yahweh's invitation to come close incorporates a whole body experience. Yahweh designed the whole sacrificial experience in a way that embodies all the senses: smell, sight, touch,

---

1. The Hebrew word *qorban* appears as a New Testament Easter egg in Mark: "But you say that if anyone tells his father or mother, 'Whatever help you would have received from me is corban' (that is, a gift for God)" (Mark 7:11 NET).

taste—that whole other half of the brain. Not just the cognitive half.

Hospitality was a big deal in the ancient culture in which Israel and her neighbours lived; sharing a meal with someone carried a lot of weight. In the ancient Near East, a host would eagerly lavish food on his guests, wash their feet, feed their animals, provide protection, and insist that they stay the night, often offering his own bed. And once a meal had been shared, a solid bond existed between them. If two parties wanted to demonstrate peace, trust, loyalty, and friendship, sharing a meal was a firm way to establish this relationship. The very first time the word *sacrifice (zebah)* is used in the Bible, it is within this precise scenario. Jacob and his father-in-law Laban didn't really see eye to eye, their relationship tarnished by deceit and dispute. But in an attempt to repair the damage, they made a pact—a covenant—promising not to harm each other. And to formalise the covenant, "Jacob offered a sacrifice on the mountain, and called his relatives to the meal; and they ate the meal" (Gen 31:54 NASB).

Now imagine if Yahweh wanted to express his relationship with his people. Inviting them to his table, inviting them to share a meal, seems the obvious and culturally appropriate way to go about it.

We don't really have a good modern day example, at least not in the culture in which I've grown up. But as I think about an Israelite bringing his gift to the doorway, the entrance to Yahweh's tent (Lev 1:3, 17:5), I remember nervously approaching the door of my girlfriend's house to meet her parents for the first time. I brought a gift: a box of chocolates. I hoped they would accept me. Would they like me? Did they like chocolate? I guess I was about to find out.

Israel didn't have to guess. Yahweh gave them specific instructions around the kinds of gifts he liked receiving, with an assurance that they *would* be accepted.

> If his offering is a burnt offering from the herd, he shall bring it near, a male without blemish; he shall bring it near to the doorway of the tent of meeting, that he may be accepted before Yahweh. (Lev 1:3)

I didn't end up marrying that girl, but it had nothing to do with my chocolates or her parents (they loved me). Don't feel sorry for me though; I ended up meeting the girl of my dreams, and pretty soon we were planning our wedding. If you've ever been involved in wedding plans, I'm sure you can relate to how much more effort goes into the wedding reception compared to the church service. The seating arrangements, selecting a menu, chicken or fish, the kind of cake, should Phil be allowed to cut the cake with his butcher's knife . . . ? A Western wedding celebration is a ritual that hasn't strayed too far from its ancient origins. Vows are exchanged. Promises are made. Two people enter into a covenantal relationship. And after the vows? That's right, a meal. Two families are united, and the coming together of the two is ritualised as the newly united family and friends share a meal together.

If sharing a meal symbolises fellowship and represents re-lationship, it's no wonder Yahweh gets so angry when his people decide to offer sacrifices to other gods. He tells them they are to stop sacrificing in the fields, and that they must now bring all of-ferings to him at his tent. The King James Version has a "cute" way of expressing Yahweh's displeasure: "They shall no more offer their sacrifices unto devils, after whom they have gone a whoring" (Lev 17:7 KJV). Yahweh's strong language is warranted, because a sacrifice is seeking communion with a god, and Israel was essentially trying to unite herself to a false god.

But Yahweh is not a false god. He is the God of Life. The reasons for wanting to *come close* to the God of Life go all the way back to Genesis. Adam and Eve walked with God. They dwelt together, and they shared an intimate relationship, but when Adam and Eve started playing with death, they had to vacate the garden and the closeness they had experienced with Yahweh. Adam and Eve were driven out—removed from direct access to the tree of life and God the Source of Life. We could say that the hope of the biblical story is for humanity to be reunited with the Source of Life, and to experience the restoration of that garden-like relationship. And Leviticus is an essential chapter in this hopeful story. Leviticus shows what must happen so that humans can once again *come close* to the Source of Life, and what it looks like to have the God of Life dwell in the midst of humanity.

One day, however, we do find out what it looks like to have the God of Life dwell in the midst of humanity.

> I am the way, and the truth, and the *life*. No one comes to the Father except through me. (John 14:6 ESV, emphasis added)

One day Jesus shows up saying, "The kingdom of God has drawn near" (Mark 1:15 BLB). And this changes everything. Not only has God *drawn near* to us but through Jesus we have been invited to draw near to God, to *come to the Father*. Formerly a Levitical priest was the only way to draw near to God, but now our high priest Jesus is the way we come to our Father. "Therefore let us draw near with confidence to the throne of grace" (Heb 4:16).

But it's not all beer and skittles. Not yet. Leviticus lays out a multitude of reasons why an Israelite could *not* draw near to God: reasons as mundane as menstruation, sex, giving birth, skin disease, touching a dead body. These circumstances aren't acts of moral failure, they are not evil, yet they prevent an Israelite from approaching God. It seems there is something about simply *being human* that must be remedied to realise Yahweh's desire to dwell with humanity.

Bonus Chapter: How Can the Sin Offering Cleanse Contamination?

IMAGINE IF I TURNED up to your birthday party in my butcher clothes, blood on my apron, fat on my boots. Can you hear the horrified gasps, feel the piercing looks of disgust? I mean, I haven't broken any laws, and, technically, legally, I haven't done anything wrong. Nevertheless, within my culture my actions are highly inappropriate.

As a second-year apprentice my days were spent almost entirely making sausages. I made so many sausages I could link them with my eyes closed. My favourite sausages were pork and honey, but unfortunately if I was an ancient Israelite I couldn't place pork and honey sausages on God's altar, for two reasons. Pork was unclean and couldn't be touched. And honey, too, was an inappropriate condiment for God's table. What's wrong with honey? And why was it okay for ancient priests to splash blood around God's tent, but you won't let me come to your birthday with blood on my apron?

Sometimes impurity makes sense, like in Deuteronomy, where they are told to bury their excrement "since Yahweh your God walks in the midst of your camp" (Deut 23:12–14). Sometimes it appears to make no sense at all, like the prohibition on including honey with an offering, or touching a cute rabbit (Lev 2:11, 11:6). But even today the lines between *impure* and *inappropriate* often don't make sense—we have our own implicit and often nonsensical cultural purity laws. Like, it's okay to clean your teeth in the bathroom, but it's not okay to eat in there. In some cultures it's rude to slurp your soup, while in Japan slurping soup is a sign you're having a good time. In the same way, it would be inappropriate for an Israelite to bring honey to God's table, or to approach God after being in contact with a dead body. Honey isn't bad, and going to a funeral isn't wrong, but before *coming close*, it was necessary to wash, wait till evening, and *then* they were considered clean and in an appropriate state to visit Yahweh (Lev 11:40).

Many scholars notice creation contains clues as to why certain things were considered unclean.[1] When God created the universe he put everything in its proper place. He separated light from dark. He separated the waters in the sky from the waters on the ground. He gave the oceans a boundary, dividing them from

1. Especially John H. Walton, who has written extensively on order, disorder, and chaos as categories within the ancient Near East.

the dry ground. He put the sky creatures in the skies. He placed the land creatures on the ground. He plopped the sea creatures into the waters.

These details have led me (and others) to conclude that when something had stepped outside of its intended order, or had strayed outside its domain, *this* is when it was considered unclean. Sex fluid on the outside? Life has leaked out. Losing blood during menstruation? Blood belongs on the inside. A leprous skin disease that causes blistered and bleeding skin appears as if it is seeping outside of its skin barrier. Mould doesn't belong inside a house. A sea creature that walks on dry land: unclean! A sky creature that walks on the ground with wings that don't work: an abomination! Creeping, crawling, underground creatures that venture up into the daylight: detestable! (Lev 11:12, 20, 29).

Vultures and ravens were also unclean, possibly because of their diet, being scavengers who feed on animal carcasses, while other birds like the buzzard, the falcon, and the owl may have been unclean because they kill creatures for food (Lev 11:13–19). Of all the things outside their symbolic domain, these birds point to something that is less of a symbol and more of a real rupture in God's ordered creation. This cause of impurity is the scandalous subject of the next chapter. Death.

But before we get there, why does slipping outside your proper domain mean you can't enter God's holy presence? There are a few ways to answer that question, and I'll get to them later in the book. Briefly here though, it may be God's way of acknowledging that some things are no longer in their intended state. Ritual impurity laws were pointing forward to the day when everything will be put back in its proper place, restored and made whole again. This is what it will look like when God and humanity dwell together. In the meantime, God is teaching his people to notice all the things that might have crept outside their proper domain, and to see this as a reminder that there are parts of the world that are currently not as God intended. From something as mundane as mould in a house, or blood on the outside, to something more devastating. Were the ocean to decide to break its shoreline: devastation.[2] Cancer cells inside your body: they don't belong there. Anything leading to loss of life is a reminder that God's intended state is life.

For Hebrew people, impurity may have been a barrier to visiting Yahweh. For us today, though, it is a message of assurance: a message informing us not of what we *must* be like but of what we *will* be like.

---

2. He set a boundary for the sea so that the water would not violate his command (Prov 8:29 NASB).

I remember sitting in class as an apprentice, being warned about the dangers of cross contamination. You can't cut chicken on the same bench as beef or lamb, otherwise people might die. Knives and benches have to be thoroughly sanitised before preparing cooked products, or else some child may get very sick. Even storing raw meat in the same fridge as cooked meat increases the risk of contamination. This is because there are dangerous contaminants which can spread unseen throughout the whole cool room, infecting everything. In the same way, impurity would also spread throughout the Israelite camp: a drifting, invisible vapour infecting anyone and anything in the vicinity.

This is the thing about impurity: it is contagious. A high priest wasn't immune; he was even considered unclean by simply stepping into the same room as a dead body. In Num 19:13 there is a warning that anyone who touches a dead body, *but does not cleanse themselves*, has defiled Yahweh's tent. Apparently Israel's impurity could spread so far that it would contaminate the altar; it could even seep under the curtain into the most holy place and infect the mercy seat. And this is a problem; if impurity was so easily transmitted, how could Yahweh remain living in the midst of an impure people, if someone could accidentally contaminate Yahweh's tent just by attending a funeral?

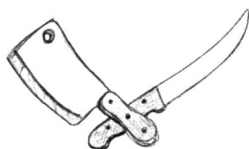

THE SIN OFFERING

Once I progressed past making sausages I began boning out legs of lamb. Finally, I got to use my brand new boning knife. My boning knife is for removing bones. When you *weed* the garden, what are you doing? Removing weeds. When you *dust* the shelves, what are you doing? Removing dust. In Lev 8, Moses performed a similar action when he took some blood and with his finger put some of it on the horns of the altar, and *sinned* the altar (Lev 8:15). Most translations use the word *purified* but the word is actually *sin*. When Moses *sinned* the altar, what was he doing? Removing sin! He was basically *de-sinning* the altar. This is why some Bible translations call the sin offering the purification offering, because essentially it is a *de-sinning* offering. As a butcher, my boning knife is for removing bones, my duster is for removing dust, and the sin offering is for removing sin.[3]

It could be a little concerning to notice some of the reasons why a person might need to be "de-sinned" and offer a sin offering: touching a dead body (Lev 5:2), giving birth (12:6), having a skin disease (14:19), a bodily discharge (15:15). Does this make you uncomfortable? Is giving birth a sin? Does having a skin disease make you a sinner?

> *I am an ancient Israelite. I have just given birth. I must bring a sin offering to Yahweh. Am I morally corrupt?*
> *I am an ancient Israelite. I accidentally put my foot on a scorpion in my Crocs. I am now required to offer a sin offering. Am I a dirty sinner?*

A Levitical priest, while shaking his head at your choice of footwear, would answer those distressing questions with an emphatic "No!" then gently offer a reassuring prescription: "The priest shall next offer the sin offering and make atonement for the one to be cleansed from his uncleanness" (Lev 14:19). The priest's prescription, Yahweh's way of dealing with this apparent impurity, is to provide cleansing!

---

3. This helpful analogy for the sin offering came from the great book by Abby Kaplan, *Misreading Ritual*, 165.

I've heard it said that God invented the sin offering to keep reminding Israel of how sinful they were. I've heard it said that the death of an animal was to remind sinful Israel that sin results in death. I've heard it said that the death of the animal is reflective of the punishment that Israel deserved.

Imagine you're an Israelite girl, not long married, still a teenager, terrified because you've gone into early labour. The pain is unbearable; how can anyone survive this much pain!? And the blood—so much blood! The midwife grips your hand, and places a messy bundle of arms and legs on your chest. But your relief turns to overwhelming panic as the midwife says the unbelievable . . .

Imagine the crippling chaos of feelings that would crush your soul: you've just given birth to a beautiful baby boy, who now lies dead on your chest. Imagine the unbearable anguish of guilt: What did I do wrong? Did I kill my baby?

Now, not only have you given birth, you've also touched a dead body, and so you know a sin offering is required. You think God is telling you that what you have done deserves punishment. Something has to die for your sin. On top of the grief of losing your baby, on top of the pervasive guilt: *Did I kill my baby? God's anger is burning against me because I have sinned.*

That is a devastating and harmful way to see the sin offering, but unfortunately sacrifice has all too often been portrayed as a retributive payment for sin.[4] But that is grossly unfair, and a tragic misrepresentation not only of what a sin offering is but also of what our God is like.

Instead, imagine a God who is gracious and compassionate, slow to anger, abounding in loving devotion and faithfulness; God in his great mercy offers a way, perhaps only a first step, but a symbolic way of removing the burden. God knows that there are things outside his intended order—pain during childbirth, grief, guilt, shame, death—and God provides the sin offering as a tactile way, a visceral ritual to help remove that burden. A careful reading of Leviticus shows that God's desire for this girl is to *cleanse* her.

> But if she cannot afford a lamb, then she shall take two turtledoves or two young doves, the one as a burnt offering and the other as a sin [purification] offering; and the priest shall make atonement for her, *and she will be clean.* (Lev 12:8 NASB, emphasis added)

Being unclean does not mean you have sinned. Being unclean or "impure" is the way Leviticus acknowledges that the world in which we live is currently not as God intended. Scholars make a distinction between *moral* impurity and *ritual* impurity, and that's a helpful distinction to have as you marinate your mind in Leviticus. We'll talk more about moral sin shortly, but what I'm pointing out here is that God's way of cleaning up the mess is the same for both ritual *and* moral impurity. Pain during childbirth, losing blood, broken bones, mental illness, foreign cancer cells in your lungs, all

---

4. Imagine saying the following to a teenage girl who has just lost her baby: "Sacrifice in the Bible, however, is the bloody reality of a bellowing animal being butchered on an altar. . . . Imagine the emotional and spiritual impact of offering this sacrifice, knowing that it was your sin that made this death necessary. . . . When you slit that animal's throat and watched it burn, and the priest declared your sin forgiven, imagine the sense of relief you felt. You would think, *It should be me. I am the one who deserves to die.*" Guthrie, "Provision of Sacrifice."

of this is outside God's good created order. Likewise, if someone commits a sin, if they break an oath, or fail to testify as a witness (Lev 5:1, 4), this also falls outside God's intended order. However, Leviticus cleans up this sort of sinful mess in the same way, stating that "the priest shall make atonement for him concerning his sin which he hath sinned in one of these, and it shall be forgiven him" (Lev 5:13 DBY[5]). God's cleanup procedure after all these messes, moral *or* ritual, is enacted through the same symbolic sin offering: "it is a sin offering" (5:12), *removing sin* and providing cleansing.

And so, no, this poor teenage Israelite girl isn't offering a sin offering because she has sinned. Yes, the sin offering removes sin, but I've found it helpful for my modern Western mind to think of the sin offering more as removing the *effects* of sin,[6] broadly understood as anything outside God's intended order. Burying your dead baby is obviously outside God's intended order. Through the sin offering, Yahweh acknowledges that sometimes tragic things happen with devastating consequences, and he provides a symbolic way of dealing with the messy aftermath, while pointing forward to a future reality where everything will be put right.

And this, dearest reader, is why I'm so passionate about Leviticus. Because, sadly, some (like the footnote above) want to see sacrifice as a payment required by God, turning it into a transaction. But this severely misrepresents God's character. In contrast to Israel's pagan neighbours, Yahweh's sacrifices sit within a covenantal relationship—a way to draw near and visit Yahweh. Rather than an imposed burden, the sin offering is a welcome invitation to draw near, to come close and experience cleansing.

---

5. Scripture quotations marked (DBY) are taken from the Darby Bible, published in 1867, 1872, 1884, 1890. This version of the Bible is in the public domain.

6. According to Robert Alter, "The context makes clear enough that an offence [sin] offering is a sacrifice that removes the effects of the offence." Alter, *Hebrew Bible*, 382–83, footnote on Lev 4:3.

And so, I wonder, when God shows up, walking among humanity, would he avoid impurity? Would he be concerned about unclean people? Would he clean up moral impurity and ritual impurity in the same way?

Remember how a high priest could not be in the same room as a dead body without becoming unclean? Luke tells about a time when Jesus entered the house of a dead girl. He walked right in, reached out, and "took her by the hand . . . and her spirit returned, and she got up immediately" (Luke 8:54–55 NASB).

Luke intentionally intertwines this story with an account of an impure woman, weaving both stories together to demonstrate what happens when Jesus encounters impurity. Jesus was on his way to the girl's house when "a woman who had suffered a chronic flow of blood . . . came up behind Him and touched the fringe of His cloak, and immediately her bleeding stopped" (Luke 8:43–44 NASB). This woman, who had been living in a state of impurity for twelve years, reached out and touched Jesus, and she was restored to wholeness. Contact with a holy God resulted in her body being "immediately healed," removing the cause of her impurity.

According to Leviticus, that woman shouldn't have been mingling. She shouldn't have risked making others impure (Lev 15:19). She was supposed to isolate and wait. In the same way, a man with a leprous skin disease could not approach Yahweh's tent in his impurity. He also had to isolate and wait, hoping to be healed or to somehow recover (Lev 13:45–46). Only *after* he had been healed could he approach a priest, who would then cleanse him. "The priest shall then take some of the blood of the guilt offering, and the priest shall put it on the lobe of the right ear of the one to be cleansed" (Lev 14:14). Luke, however, tells about a man with a leprous skin disease who, like the bleeding woman, did *not* have to wait: "When he saw Jesus, he fell on his face and begged Him, say-ing, 'Lord, if You are willing, You can make me clean'" (Luke 5:12). And Jesus "reached out with His hand and touched him, saying, 'I am willing; be cleansed'" (Luke 5:13 NASB).

Wait a minute, was this man cleansed or healed? I wonder if Jesus' response would be *what's the difference*? Is Jesus' cleansing procedure different for moral impurity and ritual impurity? Luke tells yet another story, except this time Jesus encounters a para-lysed man, and this man was *not* unclean. Nevertheless, Jesus first forgives his sins, proclaiming, "Your sins are forgiven" (5:20 NIV). Jesus then proceeds to heal his body, demonstrating that healing and forgiveness are intertwined.

Two chapters later, Jesus repeats those same words: "Your sins are forgiven" (7:48 NIV). This time, however, he is address-ing a morally impure woman, a "sinner" (7:37). This woman also experiences a *de-sinning*, Jesus demonstrating that what a sick man and an "immoral woman" need are exactly the same thing. Both need sin removed. Both need to be cleansed.

Through his actions, Jesus embodies what the sin offering was pointing to; he acknowledges that impurity, chronic bleeding, being paralysed, skin disease, and death are not part of God's ideal ordered creation. But rather than recoiling in horror, Jesus reaches out and restores the impure to wholeness.

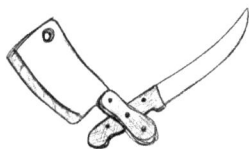

We can't leave sin alone just yet, because there's something else that needs clearing up. There was no sacrifice for wilful wrong-doing, or what the Bible calls *high-handed sin*. If someone was un-repentant in their sin, they were in danger of . . . well, let me offer an example from the butcher shop. For a while, I worked in the meat department of a big supermarket. Every morning I would walk along the cabinet tidying up the packets of meat and making a list of what needed to be prepped to fill the holes. Anything that was approaching its use-by date, or any steaks that looked a little dodgy, would get thrown into a tub, which would then get thrown into the mincer, along with the rest of the day's mince meat. Most of the time this was fine, but if an especially smelly steak found its way into the mince tub, the whole batch of mince could become corrupted. Instead of being a nice bright red, the mince might be dull and sickly looking, and the whole batch could have a slightly offensive aroma. If you're a butcher, meat may be an adequate metaphor, but the Bible prefers yeast as a metaphor for sin. Warning of the dangers of virulent teaching, Jesus says, "Beware of the yeast of the Pharisees and Sadducees" (Matt 16:6 NLT). This, perhaps, is why Leviticus says, "No grain offering that you present to the LORD is to be made with yeast, for you are not to burn any yeast or honey as a food offering to the LORD" (Lev 2:11 CSB).[7]

When Moses de-sinned the altar he *removed* the sin and impurity from an already infected surface. But persistent wrongdoing had to be cut off at the source. And so someone sinning with a high hand, refusing to repent, might also need to be cut off.

> I myself will set my face against him and will cut him off
> from his people; for by sacrificing his children to Molek,
> he has defiled my sanctuary and profaned my holy name.
> (Lev 20:3 NIV)

In Leviticus, there is no sacrifice available for a high-handed sinner, which further highlights how a sacrifice cannot be transactional. A proudly unrepentant sinner could not expect to offer a sacrifice and be cleansed, because sacrifice does not address the problem of the offerer's heart. You see, sacrifice is supposed to be an expression of the offerer's inner heart. Like one rotten piece of meat contaminating the whole tub, a problem person persisting in sin had to be removed to keep the whole camp clean. Removing a

---

7. It's not a slam dunk, however. While yeast is never burned on the altar, yeast *is* presented with other offerings: "Bring two loaves of bread from your settlements as a presentation offering, each of them made from four quarts of fine flour, baked with yeast, as firstfruits to the LORD" (Lev 23:17 CSB).

part to keep the whole clean is a very biblical pattern. In Deuteronomy, God reveals his plan to cure a contaminated heart.

> The LORD your God will circumcise your heart and the hearts of your descendants, to love the LORD your God with all your heart and all your soul, so that you may live. (Deut 30:6 NASB)

"So that you may live," Yahweh says he will circumcise your heart, removing only a part. There's an awfully important detail to notice, especially if you're a circumcision doctor: circumcision by definition only removes a part, not the whole thing.[8]

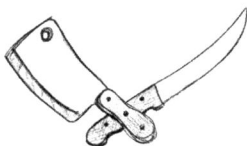

While the death of a high-handed sinner might be necessary to remove the *cause* of the impurity, one surprising and often overlooked detail is that God can clean up sin without anything dying. Neither is a death necessary for forgiveness. Leviticus says quite explicitly, "If his means are insufficient for two turtledoves or two young doves, then for his offering for that which he has sinned, he shall bring the tenth of an ephah of fine flour as a sin offering. . . . It is a sin offering" (Lev 5:11 NASB). No death. No blood. Only flour. Yet forgiveness and atonement are still provided.

And so, on that note, let's talk about death.

---

8. Circumcision comes from the Latin, meaning *cut around*.

Six: What's Significant About Slaughter?

I HAVE TO TELL you something. And I'm not going to mince my words. I'm still bitter that you wouldn't let me attend your birthday party with blood on my clothes. Because did you know that a priest was not allowed to serve in sacred space *unless* he had blood wiped onto his clothing (Lev 8:30)? Perhaps you'd be happier if, after working with animal carcasses, I went home, had a shower, and changed my clothes? Well, in the same way, but a little confoundingly, if a Hebrew touched an unclean animal carcass, he could not visit Yahweh until later that night after he had washed his clothes: "Whoever picks up any of their carcasses shall wash his clothes and be unclean until evening" (Lev 11:25).

Well, the conundrum continues, because a lamb could be brought to Yahweh's tent, slaughtered, and placed on his altar, but if that same lamb died in the field, or in a shepherd's arms, that shepherd was unclean and could *not* come close to Yahweh's tent.

> If an animal that you are allowed to eat dies, anyone who touches its carcass will be unclean till evening. (Lev 11:39 NIV)

Why were the pieces of an offering considered clean and pure enough to be placed on Yahweh's holy altar, but a person was unclean, and could not approach the altar if they'd touched an animal carcass?

> And if one touches anything made unclean by a corpse, . . . a person who touches any such thing shall be unclean until evening and shall not eat of the holy gifts unless he

has bathed his body in water. But the sun will set, and he will be clean. And afterward he shall eat of the holy gifts, for it is his food. He shall not eat an animal which dies or is torn by beasts, becoming unclean by it; I am Yahweh. (Lev 22:4–8)

An animal that died in the field couldn't be brought near to God as an offering. A priest who had come into contact with a dead body couldn't serve in sacred space. A high priest and a Nazirite couldn't even be in the same room as their dead parents without becoming unclean, rendering themselves unable to visit Yahweh: "He must not go near any dead person or make himself unclean even for his father or mother" (Lev 21:11 CSB).

Ezekiel talks about the temple being defiled by the dead bodies of humans. "Defile the temple and fill the courtyards with the dead" (Ezek 9:7 NASB). Numbers emphasises the aversion to contact with death, saying, "Anyone who is defiled by a dead body . . . send them outside the camp so they will not defile their camp, where I dwell among them" (Num 5:2–3 BSB[1]). Are you seeing the pattern? Everything death-related was ritualised by keeping it away from God's dwelling place, often sending it outside the camp. To cut to the chase: death could not exist in God's presence. Death and Yahweh, the God of Life, coexisting in the same space should be something of an oxymoron, and we're about to see why.

In the second chapter, we saw that an animal carcass was never given to God and a corpse was never placed on his altar. It was important to establish that first, because it helps explain our current conundrum. Placing pieces of meat onto Yahweh's altar is not bringing death into his presence. Bringing near an offering is not bringing near a dead animal. Nothing to do with death is brought into sacred space.

Leviticus 10 tells the story of Nadab and Abihu, who brought impure fire into God's presence, "and they died before Yahweh" (v. 2). What do you suppose has to happen now that death has

1. The Holy Bible, Berean Standard Bible, (BSB) produced in cooperation with Bible Hub, Discovery Bible, OpenBible.com, and the Berean Bible Translation Committee. This version of the Bible is in the public domain.

been brought into Yahweh's presence? It has to be removed. And this is precisely what happens. God instructs the priests, "Carry your relatives away from the front of the sanctuary to the outside of the camp" (Lev 10:4). A similar eviction occurred in another of God's dwelling places. Adam and Eve got themselves mixed up with death, eating from a tree of which God said, *if you eat of it you will die*. And so the humans were sent outside the garden, away from the tree of life, and away from the Source of Life.

When these humans were sent out of the garden they exited to the east, and God placed cherubim to guard the way back in. In the same way, the doorway to the tent faced east, which meant as the priest proceeded through the courtyard, into the most holy place, he was heading west, back towards God's presence, the way in guarded by cherubim sewn into the dividing curtain. Near the centre of the tent, a tree-like lampstand gave light, described as having branches, bulbs, flowers, and blossoms. The high priest sewed pomegranates around the hem of his robe, as though he was working in a garden of fruit and abundance. Why do you suppose the priest wore an ephod of gold with onyx stones? Well, obviously because onyx stones and gold were plentiful in the garden in Eden (Gen 2:12, Exod 28:6, 9). Leviticus 26 even reiterates God's promise to his people to make them fruitful and multiply them, that he will dwell among them and walk among them, using the same word for when God walked in the garden (Gen 3:8). "So I will turn toward you and make you fruitful and multiply you. . . . I will make My dwelling among you. . . . I will also walk among you and be your God, and you shall be My people" (Lev 26:9–12).

This is why death couldn't come close to the tent; because Yahweh's tent stands in the centre of the camp as a beacon of life, a fertile garden space in the midst of a wilderness, with the Source of Life himself dwelling at the centre. And everything about the tent was carefully crafted to teach Israel that God was inviting them back into an Eden-like relationship.

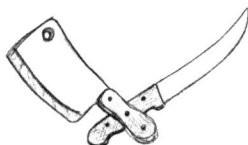

Okay, this is a chapter on slaughter, so we should stop trying to avoid death. Very little instruction is given for how the animal is to be killed, however. Ritual is hugely important to ancient sacrifice. And so it should strike you as peculiar that there are almost no ritualistic instructions around the slaughter at all. And any instructions there are, are vastly outweighed by instructions on blood application and eating. One time, I counted all the instructions for slaughter, and compared them to the instructions for what to do with the blood. The ratio was more than three-to-one, blood to slaughter. Then I counted all the instructions on eating the offerings—where to eat the offering, who eats it, which bits to eat, when to eat it, which bits not to eat—and the results were the same: more than three-to-one in favour of food. You might be wondering what kind of knife to use, what words to recite, or how to secure the animal, but Leviticus doesn't consider these details important. Remarkably, the only specific instruction around the killing is that it be killed to the north side of the altar, or simply "before the Lord" (Lev 1:5, 11 NIV). Sometimes, as with the guilt offering, any instruction around the killing is left out completely (5:14–19).

One thing we can be sure of is that in most cases the person bringing the offering performs the slaughter, not the priest, and this is important. Everything that is ritualised is highly symbolic, and the priests are acting as God's divine representatives. And so if the death was supposed to convey some symbolic meaning—perhaps someone wants to suggest that the animal was dying a God-ordained death, or receiving a death penalty imposed by God—we would expect the priest to perform the slaughter on behalf of Yahweh as his representative. But this is not part of the process.

Whatever symbolism the slaughter may communicate, the offerer is the one holding the knife.

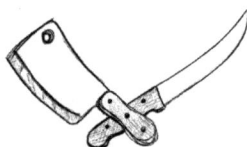

Normally the driver unloads the beef quarters one at a time. Two forequarters. Two hindquarters. Because even gutted, skinned, and quartered, they are quite heavy.[2] While I have never attempted to deadlift a live bull, try to picture the absurdity of wrangling a live bull up onto the altar. How the heck would anyone pick up a live bull? Add to this the obvious but often overlooked fact that the altar was always burning: "Fire shall be kept burning continually on the altar; it shall not go out" (Lev 6:13). Who would ever consider trying to manoeuvre a live bull into the midst of the flames, hold it there, and then reach into the flames with a knife?

2. Composed in the second century BC, the "Letter of Aristeas" recounts a visit to the temple, where Aristeas admiringly describes the priests and their skill at hurling the heavy sacrificial pieces up onto the altar: "The ministration of the priests is in every way unsurpassed both for its physical endurance and for its orderly and silent service. For they all work spontaneously, though it entails much painful exertion, and each one has a special task allotted to him. The service is carried on without interruption—some provide the wood, others the oil, others the fine wheat flour, others the spices; others again bring the pieces of flesh for the burnt offering, exhibiting a wonderful degree of strength. For they take up with both hands the limbs of a calf, each of them weighing more than two talents, and throw them with each hand in a wonderful way on to the high place of the altar and never miss placing them on the proper spot. In the same way the pieces of the sheep and also of the goats are wonderful both for their weight and their fatness. For those, whose business it is, always select the beasts which are without blemish and especially fat, and thus the sacrifice which I have described, is carried out." Aristeas, "Letter," 92–93.

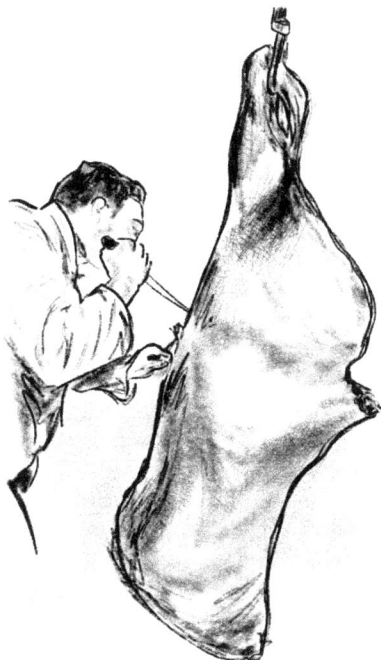

All that to say: the animal is not killed on the altar.

In the garden, talking to Adam and Eve about eating from the tree of knowing good and evil, Yahweh says, *dying, you will die.* Some people have suggested that the death of the animal in Leviticus is a call back to the death that Adam and Eve deserved. And so I looked for that word *die* in Leviticus, expecting that same word to be used to refer to the slaughter of an animal. But I searched right through Leviticus and, guess what, that word is never used to describe a sacrificial animal—not once. Intriguingly the one time the word *die is* used in reference to an animal, it's as a warning not to touch it because the carcass is unclean. "If one of the animals dies which you have for food, the one who touches its carcass becomes unclean until evening" (Lev 11:39 NIV).

> *You have been invited to your mother-in-law's home for Christmas lunch. She has asked you to bring roast pork. You arrive. You knock. And as she opens the door you*

present her with the whole carcass of a dead pig. "I brought you a dead animal!" you exclaim, as she passes out on the doorstep.

The meaning of your Thanksgiving turkey or your Christmas roast pork goes far beyond the killing of the animal. No one talks about the death of the chicken in Auntie Mabel's salad. And no one feels the need to point out the piece of dead pig on the Christmas platter, unless Uncle Dave is really struggling to carve it up: "*The pig's already dead, Dave!*" In the same way, Leviticus has much to say about ceremony and ritual, food and festival—and blood—but, just like your Thanksgiving dinner or Christmas lunch, the death is not a focal point of the proceedings. Yes, death has occurred, but the death isn't the point of the meal. Similarly, when I give my wife flowers, she doesn't normally interpret the point of my gift as a death. Yes, technically, I killed the flowers and they are now slowly dying in the vase, but only a sadist sees death as the meaning behind the gift.

In the meat industry there is a term known as DCB, which stands for "dark cutting beef." It's a phenomenon that occurs when the animal has been stressed before slaughter. If an animal is stressed, several things happen, none of them ideal. A chemical reaction known as glycolysis occurs in the muscle tissue, converting glycogen into lactic acid, and the animal experiences an increase of cortisol, a stress hormone that severely reduces meat quality. When working with this kind of meat on the butcher's block, it becomes pretty obvious if an animal had been stressed prior to slaughter. The meat appears much darker in colour, and it will have an unpleasant taste.

Something else you don't want in your steak is bruising. If I see a bruise while preparing meat I will normally discard it. It looks disgusting, and the mouthfeel is gross. Plus, it's more likely to spoil quicker due to the higher blood content. We'll talk more about bruising in the "Unblemished" chapter, but, long story short, bruises are bad, and any animal with a bruise or a broken bone or any other blemish could not be given to God.

Reassuringly, Leviticus contains no instructions to hit, beat, mock, spit at, or torture the animal. Occasionally, however, while reading scholars I admire and respect, I come across statements that don't align with the language of Leviticus.

> The violent death of the animal signifies the penalty human beings deserve for their sin. . . . The shedding of blood signifies violent death. Forgiveness only comes through the violent death of an animal.[3]

I'm sorry, but this is not what Leviticus teaches, nor is this an accurate portrayal of animal slaughter—and I'm speaking from experience. Moreover, Jewish tradition demonstrates that sacrificial slaughter was designed to be as fast and painless as possible, and anything that might cause pain, such as a nick in the slaughtering knife or a delay in the cutting, was strictly forbidden. In the Bronze Age, where animals were generally killed with spears, bows and arrows, or clubs, the strict Jewish method of slaughtering was possibly the most humane form around. In a later chapter I'll share a story about my experience of a Jewish kosher kill, but, suffice to say for now, the slaughter of a sacrificial animal can in no way represent some kind of violent punishment, or retributive penalty.

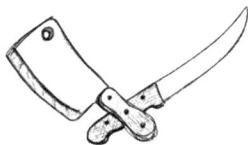

---

3. Schreiner, "Substitutionary Atonement," para. 7.

I'm sorry if I've left you dying for more, but if you're look-ing for some kind of deeper meaning behind sacrificial slaughter, you may have to look outside Leviticus. Lamentably, I don't believe Leviticus allows us to elevate the significance of the death of an animal any higher without the risk of inserting our own bias.

On the bright side, however, if a *death* is not what defines sacrifice, then perhaps a *living* sacrifice will cease to become an oxymoron.

Therefore, I urge you, brothers and sisters, in view of God's mercy, to offer your bodies as a living sacrifice, holy and pleasing to God. (Rom 12:1 NIV)

First, notice the sequence: sacrifice is a response, offered *after* and as a *reaction* to God's mercy. Notice also what is plural and what is singular. Bodies is plural. Sacrifice is singular. Paul is addressing the Roman church, a sprawling, multiethnic, diverse, and dysfunctional family. But Paul, insisting that this family is to be *united*, urges them to offer their many bodies, as one living sacrifice.

The Roman church was made up of many different members: multiethnic gentiles, Jews, men, women, rich, poor, slave, free. Yet they were united, because they were Christ's body. And this is precisely what Paul says next: "For just as each of us has one body with many members, and these members do not all have the same function, so in Christ we, though many, form one body" (Rom 12:4–5 NIV).

We are the body of Christ. And as Christ's body, we participate with him and *in* him. In everything. His death. His life. His resurrection. His rule.[4] And as members of Christ's body, our unified actions are accepted by God as a living sacrifice—a gift, holy and pleasing.

---

4. Eph 2:5–6; Rom 6:4–5, 7:4; Gal 2:20; Col 2:12–13; 2 Tim 2:11–12; Rev 3:21.

Seven: Why Is Fat Off the Table?

THIS IS THE CULPRIT chapter. Two topics within this chapter finally prompted me to merge meat with my long lost love of writing.

My current passion for biblical studies didn't begin in Leviticus. It began with atonement. It actually began several years ago when someone made a throwaway remark about Jesus' death on the cross that was true. I *knew* it was true because of the many biblical studies classes I'd endured at school. However, when I tried to find that "truth" in the Bible, it wasn't there. That's a long story for another time, but the upshot is this: I thought I knew the Bible pretty well, but I'd just discovered a gaping hole in my "knowledge." And the more I dug, the more it revealed just how big that hole had been the whole time. Nevertheless, I kept digging. As I went down, down deep into the wombat warren of atonement, I tunnelled sideways and discovered the forgotten cave of ancient sacrifice. And this led me into the cavernous and glorious world of Leviticus.

One day as I was exploring the hidden depths of Leviticus, unearthing treasures and finding hidden gems and precious stones, I came across kidneys and livers. I was reading a book called *Leviticus as Literature* by Mary Douglas, and she observed how a lamb's anatomy can be seen as analogous to the tabernacle. That day two things happened: as I read about the significance of kidneys being in the centre of the animal, I thought, "I've removed enough kidneys in my time to know that, yes, they really *are* in the centre." And when I read about livers being heavy, I thought, "Yeah, livers *are* surprisingly heavy." And *then* I thought, why not reawaken my love of literature by writing about the butchering of beasts from a butcher's perspective.

All fat is Yahweh's. (Lev 3:16)

Under my bench are two tubs: a fat tub and a bone tub. Occasionally a customer asks for a bone to take home to their dog, but usually the bones are picked up by the fat and bone truck, to be ground up for pet food, fertiliser, or gelatin. All excess fat goes into the fat tub, to be collected and turned into soap or biofuel, but this would have horrified an ancient Hebrew, because fat was considered the best bit.

The fatty portions, or *suet*[1] in some translations, was a prized delicacy on an ancient dinner table. Abel was the first to bring the "fat portions" (Gen 4:4) or the *choicest morsels* with his offering, essentially giving God his best. Later on, *fat* becomes a term that describes the best and most sumptuous portions of all produce; thus we read "the fat of the land" (Gen 45:18 NIV) and "the fat of wheat," which basically means the finest produce or the best wheat (Pss 81:16; 147:14 YLT). Leviticus stresses that these fatty portions are reserved for Yahweh alone. No one is allowed to eat the fat, because all fat belongs to Yahweh (Lev 7:22–25).

1. Suet is the thick white fat that covers the kidneys of cattle, sheep, and goats. It runs along the backbone along the centre of the loins.

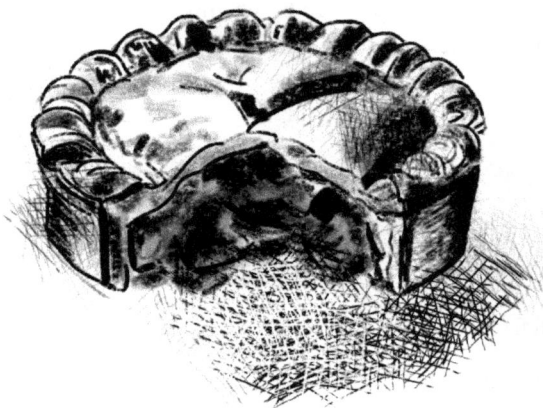

One of my responsibilities as an apprentice, which was very repetitive but very satisfying, was to remove the kidneys from the lambs. The kidneys are encased in a thick covering of fat, and by the time the lambs arrive in our cool room, the fat has hardened. I would pluck the kidneys out and discard the fat, horrifying our ancient Hebrew friends. Then I'd dice the kidneys up, combined with some diced beef, and lo and behold, steak and kidney. When looking inside an animal, the kidneys and the other internal organs, along with the protective layer of fat, are quite obviously in the middle, at the very centre of the animal's being.[2]

Let's consider kidneys: "My inmost being will rejoice when your lips speak what is right" (Prov 23:16 NIV). Those words, *inmost being*, are actually one word, and that one word is . . . *kidneys*. Again, "When my soul was embittered, when I was pricked in heart" (Ps 73:21 RSV). Poor Asaph wasn't pricked in his heart at all; he was pricked in his *kidneys*. *Inmost being* and *heart* aren't totally terrible translations, because in Hebrew imagination the kidneys were regarded as expressing the deepest inner affections and character. Whether your kidneys are pricked or rejoicing, your kidneys are conveying the kind of joy and pain experienced at a deeply emotional level.

2. See illustration on page 57.

Now let's look at livers. Around the ninth century AD, a group of Jewish scholars known as the Masoretes codified the Hebrew Bible, meticulously adding vowel points to help with pronunciation, as the original Hebrew contains no vowels. When they got to Gen 49:6, the Masoretes must have paused at the Hebrew word *KVD*, knowing that, depending on where they placed the vowel points, that three letter word could be pronounced either *kaved* or *kavod*. The Masoretes decided to go with *kavod*, or *glory*. However, the Septuagint, the Greek Translation of the Old Testament, which was translated in the third century BC, read those same Hebrew consonants and interpreted *KVD* as *kaved*, or . . . liver!

Most English translations stick with the Masoretes and *glory*, yet the NET Bible notes that the Hebrew word is more likely *liver*. I think the Septuagint got it right in this instance, because in Hebrew thought the inner organs were associated with emotions, and the liver, as the heaviest organ, became associated with the heaviest and most weighty emotions. (As a butcher I can confirm that the liver is indeed the heaviest of the internal organs.) The relationship between liver and glory appears even closer when realising that although we translate *kavod* as *glory*, it literally means *heavy*, *weighty*, or *significant*.

A fun story demonstrates this connection. Eli was a heavy man. And when Eli heard that the ark of the LORD had been captured, he fell off his chair "and he died, for he was old and heavy" (1 Sam 4:18 NASB). Eli's daughter-in-law was pregnant at the time, and when she gave birth "she named the child Ichabod, saying, 'The glory is departed from Israel'" (1 Sam 4:21 NASB). Are you cracking up? Do you get it? The name Ichabod, *i kavod*, means *glory is gone*. But it is also a hilarious play on words, because *kavod*, meaning *heavy* or *weighty*, also implies that Eli, the heavy one, has departed.[3]

Usually when the Hebrew word *liver* shows up describing emotion, English Bibles avoid it, instead using words like *heart* or *inmost being*, but some, like the KJV, leave liver as *liver*.

3. Thanks to Tim Mackie from the *BibleProject* for this gem. Mackie, "Glory," 17:19.

My bowels are troubled,
my liver is poured upon the earth. (Lam 2:11 KJV)

With all this new knowledge, if livers and kidneys were to turn up together on Yahweh's altar, would you expect it to signify deep and heavy emotion? Affections and character?

> And from it he shall bring near his offering as an offering by fire to Yahweh the fat that covers the entrails and all the fat that is on the entrails, and the two kidneys with the fat that is on them, which is on the loins, and the lobe of the liver, which he shall remove with the kidneys. And the priest shall offer them up in smoke on the altar as food, an offering by fire for a soothing aroma; all fat is Yahweh's. (Lev 3:14–16)

When an ancient Israelite looked inside an animal offering, they didn't see a blood cleanser and fluid filters, they perceived glory, intense affections, and weighty emotion. The phrase *pleasing aroma*, which is the subject of the next chapter, occurs most often with reference to these inner organs and the fat that surrounds them. These tasty morsels were not only the most desirable culinary delicacies, they were also identified with the innermost *being*. Thus, when placing liver and kidneys on the altar, this is symbolically offering up the interior being, glory, and passions of the animal as what is pleasing to God. Correspondingly, an unblemished innermost being, a flawless character, pure passions, is analogous to what pleases God in humans.[4]

---

4. Thanks to my friend Spencer Owen for providing much of the language for these links between the physical inner parts and the emotions. You should check out Spencer Owen's podcast, *Trauma-Informed Church Kid* (churchkid-pod.podbean.com).

One day Jesus was having a hearty chat with a crowd of people, when he suddenly began describing the dirty insides of some of the not-so-innocent bystanders. Some "blind" Pharisees who hadn't quite grasped the underlying lessons from Leviticus, sheepishly found themselves on the receiving end of a scathing rebuke.

> You blind Pharisee, first clean the inside of the cup and of the dish, so that the outside of it may become clean also. Woe to you, scribes and Pharisees, hypocrites! For you are like whitewashed tombs which on the outside appear beautiful, but inside they are full of dead men's bones and all uncleanness. In this way, you also outwardly appear righteous to men, but inwardly you are full of hypocrisy and lawlessness. (Matt 23:26–28)

Here is Jesus, brilliantly redefining, or rather *revealing* why all along God had given such specific instructions around what kinds of offerings were acceptable on his altar. It wasn't so much about the state of the offering—it was the state of the offerer's heart. And their liver. And their kidneys.

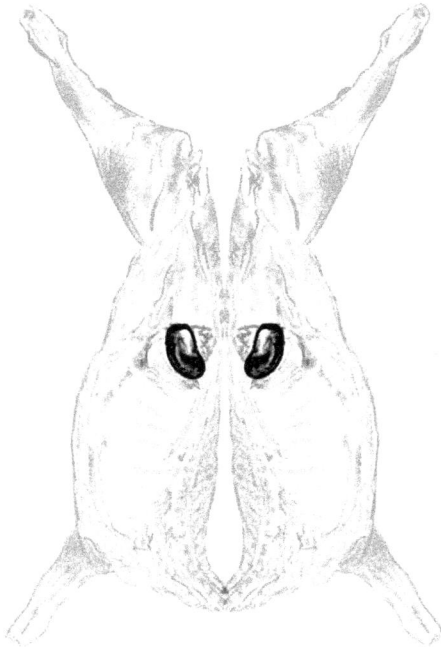

On his altar, God got all the fat: the very best bits. Likewise at his table today, he desires the very best from us. On his altar, God required unblemished livers and kidneys, but at his table today, he desires pure passions. On his altar, God required clean kidneys, but at his table today, he desires an uncorrupted character. On his altar, God required spotless livers, but at his table today, he desires deep and honest emotions.

> So if you are offering your gift at the altar, and there remember that your brother has something against you, leave your gift there before the altar and go; first be reconciled to your brother, and then come and offer your gift. (Matt 5:23–24 RSV)

Again Jesus reveals that the state of the offerer's inmost being is more important than what is placed on the altar. And Jesus uncovers the more fundamental principle behind bringing an offering: reconciliation. Jesus is basically saying, *if you are about to give God a gift, stop! Your sacrifice is worthless if you are not at peace with your brother.* Being reconciled to your neighbour is more important than sacrifice. Here I think we are hearing echoes of the guilt offering, and glimpsing principles behind the peace offering—reconciliation between members of a community, and humanity being reconciled to God. And it shouldn't really be a surprise that reconciliation trumps sacrifice; Yahweh has been saying it for years . . .

> For I desire faithful love and not sacrifice,
> the knowledge of God rather than burnt offerings. (Hos 6:6 CSB)

Eight: Is a Dead Animal Really a Pleasing Aroma?

THE TABLE IS SET, a lavish buffet to be sent up as a tantalising aroma to Yahweh: meat, bread, cakes, oil, fine flour, fatty portions, a seasoning of salt. The priest prepares the meal on the altar, the flames sear the meat, the fat begins to drip out, a big splash of wine poured over the roasting pieces, hissing and sputtering. Finally frankincense is added to the flames and the whole thing ascends in billows of fragrant smoke.

> The priest will burn the food on the altar, as a food offering for a pleasing aroma. (Lev 3:16 CSB)

The CSB and the NIV describe the aroma as *pleasing*, while other English translations prefer *soothing* or *sweet*. The Hebrew word comes from a root that means settling down or coming to rest, and has connotations of causing pleasant delight. As I alluded to earlier, it's important to notice that the phrase "pleasing aroma" nearly always occurs in conjunction with "food offerings" language. If a *food offering* on earth is reaching God's nostrils in heaven as a *pleasant aroma*, we are experiencing the coming together of heaven and earth over a meal, and surely we are being led to understand these rituals as pointing to *communion with the divine*.

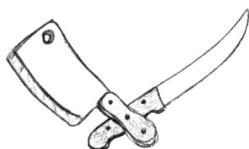

Hopefully we've already established that death didn't come into contact with God's altar, and so God wasn't receiving the death of an animal as a sweet smell. He didn't appreciate the wafting scent of death rising up into his nostrils.

You might expect the sin offering to smell bad in God's nostrils, but even this is experienced by God as a pleasant aroma (Lev 4:31). There is a flip side, however. What happens if the Israelites act in a way that causes God to turn his nose up?

> Yet if in spite of this you do not obey Me, but act with hostility against Me, then I will act with wrathful hostility against you. . . . I will turn your cities into ruins as well and make your sanctuaries desolate, and I will not smell your soothing aromas. (Lev 26:27–28, 31 NASB)

This warning reveals another important aspect of God's character: offerings to Yahweh do not have magical appeasing powers. Even if Israel was to follow all the correct procedures, offering the sacrifices properly, obeying the letter of the law so to speak, if their heart was hostile, if their motives were corrupt, Yahweh wants none of it. They can have a big barbeque and burn all the meat and incense they want, but it will never reach Yahweh's nose.

Here's how Leviticus describes an offering after it is portioned up and placed on the wood on the altar: "The priest is to burn all of it on the altar. It is a burnt offering, a food offering, an aroma pleasing to the LORD" (Lev 1:9 NIV). Notice the word order; it does not *give off* an aroma, rather the whole offering *becomes* a sweet aroma. The Jewish Publication Society (JPS) translation (1917) does a good job of conveying the transformative nature of the smoke.

> The priest shall offer the whole, and make it smoke upon the altar; it is a burnt-offering, an offering made by fire, of a sweet savour unto the LORD. (Lev 1:13 JPS)

In her book *Leviticus as Literature*, Mary Douglas further explains the challenging concept of transmogrification,[1] quoting Jacob Milgrom[2] extensively.

---

1. I have no idea what this word means; I found it in a thesaurus.

2. Jacob Milgrom wrote a massive three-volume, twenty-six-hundred-page

Milgrom notes that in Hebrew the verb "to turn into smoke" is not the same as the verb "to burn," used for non-sacrificial incineration: it means turning something into something else, smoke. In the Iliad (1: 317) the savoury odours of sacrifice mixed with curling smoke went up to the gods in the sky (Hicks 1953); in Leviticus the "offering is not destroyed but transformed into smoke, sublimated, etherealised." If the verb in this much-repeated sentence means turning everything into smoke, Milgrom is saying that the act of sacrifice is less a killing than a transformation from one kind of existence to another.[3]

---

commentary, which is widely considered to be the definitive work on Leviticus.

3. Douglas, *Leviticus as Literature*, 68.

Michael Morales, (who wrote my favourite commentary on Leviticus, *Who Shall Ascend the Mountain of the Lord?*) sees a similar transformation occurring. "The burning rite transforms the animal's flesh into a 'pleasing aroma' . . . transporting it to God's heavenly abode as the smoke ascends from the altar."[4] The suggestion being made is that the offering is being transformed from earthly matter into a *spiritual substance*. The offering transforms into "vapour" or "smoke" that ascends and then disappears into the spiritual realm, with Morales imagining it ascending into heaven itself.

To summarise, the offering does not burn up and simply disappear; rather the offering changes in essence—it transforms into smoke, an ungraspable substance associated with the spiritual realm. The offering, now a spiritual substance, is able to ascend into heaven, into God's abode as a pleasing aroma.

Now seems like as good a time as any to further flesh out the transformation that takes place on the altar when an animal or a handful of grain becomes a holy offering and ascends as smoke into Yahweh's holy heavens.

Previously we noticed that impurity had a contagious quality; a person could catch uncleanness just by being in the same room as a dead body.

But the opposite is also true.

An encounter with God could leave a lingering holiness. After Moses encountered Yahweh and spoke with him, his face shone (Exod 34:35). And, when describing the sin offering, Leviticus says, "Whatever touches any of the flesh will become holy" (Lev 6:27 NIV).

---

4. Morales, *Who Shall Ascend?*, 133.

Holiness, too, is contagious. In Exodus we are told, "The altar will be most holy, and whatever touches it will be holy" (Exod 29:37 NIV; see also 30:28–29). And later Jesus affirms that contact with the altar makes the offering holy.

> Which is greater: the gift, or the altar that makes the gift
> sacred? (Matt 23:19 NIV)

Jesus is essentially saying that the altar sanctifies the sacrifice,[5] illustrating the contagious quality of holiness. One simultaneously unnerving yet reassuring ramification of this is that when something impure comes into contact with holiness, holiness wins. Holiness is greater than impurity.

Isaiah has his own unnerving encounter with a holy altar when one day he wakes up, rolls over, and sees Yahweh sitting on his throne, with two terrifying seraphim flying around the room. Understandably, Isaiah freaks out as he realises he's not in Kansas anymore. He's not even in the earthly tent. He's in Yahweh's heavenly throne room. He shouldn't be here. He is unclean and he knows it. He waits, expecting to be consumed by fire at any moment.

> Woe is me, for I am ruined!
> For I am a man of unclean lips,
> And I live among a people of unclean lips. (Isa 6:5)

Suddenly, one of the seraphim flies ominously towards him, holding a hot coal plucked from the holy altar. He extends it towards Isaiah's lips . . . *Behold*, the seraphim says, "this has touched your lips; and your iniquity is taken away, and your sin is atoned for" (6:7).

No dead animal. No blood. Just an encounter with a holy coal from the altar, and Isaiah is cleansed and purified.

---

5. Andrew Remington Rillera makes this point in his 2024 book *Lamb of the Free: Recovering the Varied Sacrificial Understandings of Jesus's Death*.

A story is told in Acts about Peter, who falls into a trance while waiting for his dinner. In his dream he sees a sheet containing all different kinds of unclean animals *lowered by four corners to the ground,* possibly signifying the four corners of the earth and that what Peter is about to learn pertains to the whole world. A voice tells Peter to *get up, sacrifice, and eat.* Peter is indignant: "Surely not, Lord! I have never eaten anything impure or unclean." The voice speaks to him a second time, "Do not call anything impure that God has made clean" (Acts 10:14–15 NIV). Understanding that the main meaning wasn't so much regarding food, Peter immediately gets up and goes to a house full of "unclean" *people.*

> Peter went inside and found a large gathering of people. He said to them: ". . . God has shown me that I should not call anyone impure or unclean." (Acts 10:27–28 NIV)

Peter was told, "Do not call anything impure that God has made clean," and Peter's interpretation is, "I should not call any*one* impure or unclean." Peter certainly seems to be under the impression that all of humanity has been cleansed, and, if Peter is correct, the implications are astounding!

Impure humanity must have come into contact with something holy. Something or someone holy must have taken away iniquity and decontaminated the four corners of the world.

May I suggest that someone is Jesus? Jesus' power to purify is more powerful than any purification offering. Jesus' pleasing aroma is more pleasant than any animal or grain offering. And Jesus' holiness is greater than the altar's holiness. By taking on a human body, Jesus brought heaven to earth, infecting humanity with holiness. And, in his human body, Jesus fulfilled his Father's plan to "bring everything together in Christ, both things in heaven and things on earth" (Eph 1:10 CSB).

Everything. Heaven has infected every part of creation. Jesus came into contact with every part of human existence in his birth, life, death, and resurrection. Saint Athanasius (ca. AD 330) sums it up well when he says, "Not even His birth from a virgin, therefore, changed Him in any way, nor was he defiled by being in the body. Rather, he sanctified the body by being in it."[6] And Jesus did not sanctify his own body only, but ours also.

> By this will we have been sanctified through the offering of the body of Jesus Christ once for all. . . . For by one offering He has perfected for all time those who are being sanctified. (Heb 10:10, 14)

When Jesus took on a human body he united humanity to himself, incorporating humanity into the divine nature;[7] we have, according to our friend Peter, "become partakers of the divine nature" (2 Pet 1:4). And since we participate in the divine nature, we have come into contact with, and been infected with, Jesus' holiness.

> For both He who sanctifies [makes holy] and those who are being sanctified are all of One; for which reason He is not ashamed to call them brothers. (Heb 2:11)

But what would happen if Jesus came into contact with death? We already watched Jesus reach out and touch a dead girl, and immediately "her spirit returned." But what about if Jesus himself encountered death? What would happen if Jesus descended to the place of the dead?

---

6. From, possibly my favourite book ever, Athanasius, *On the Incarnation*, 17. Similarly, Saint Irenaeus (AD 180) famously wrote, "He therefore passed through every age, becoming an infant for infants, thus sanctifying infants; a child for children, thus sanctifying those who are of this age . . . a youth for youths, becoming an example to youths, and thus sanctifying them for the Lord. So likewise He was an old man for old men . . . sanctifying at the same time the aged also." Nagasawa, *Christmas with Irenaeus*, 14.

7. Thanks to Spencer Owen for crafting these words: "Humanity is assumed by (taken up into/added to) the divine nature."

He who descended is Himself also He who ascended far
above all the heavens, so that He might fill all things.
(Eph 4:10)

Jesus filled all things. Even death. Unlike a Levitical offering,
Jesus didn't deal with the mere aftereffects of impurity; Jesus cau-
terised impurity at its source, condemning sin itself (Rom 8:3), and
swallowing up death forever (Isa 25:8; 1 Cor 15:54; Heb 2:14–15).
Yet even in death, Jesus did not participate in or perpetuate the
endless cycle of death and defilement. Instead, Jesus demonstrated
without a doubt that the impurity of death had zero sticking power.
Holiness won. Holiness came into contact with death, and death
was rendered impotent.[8]

And what Jesus did, he did on behalf of all humanity, so that,
*if we died with him, we will also live with him, and we will certainly
also be united with him in a resurrection like his, because God has
raised us up and seated us in the heavenly realms in Christ* (para-
phrasing 2 Tim 2:11; Rom 6:5, 8; Eph 2:5–6).

Today though, while our feet are still on earth, Ephesians
encourages us to live like Jesus lived, to walk like Jesus walked:
"Walk in love, just as Christ also loved us and gave Himself up for
us, an offering and a sacrifice to God as a fragrant aroma" (Eph
5:2). Clearly, it wasn't Jesus' death that was a fragrant aroma in
God's nostrils. Death does not smell pleasant to God. Rather, it was
Jesus' action that was received as a sweet smelling gift, his selfless
act of giving—lovingly giving himself for us. In a sense, Jesus was
the smoke ascending to the heavens—a fragrant aroma—and as
the smoke stretched from earth to heaven, Jesus united humanity
to heaven.

And since we are being encouraged to "live a life filled with
love, following the example of Christ" (Eph 5:2 NLT), we too can

---

8. It's nice to know I'm in good company; I read the following quote from
Rillera's concluding chapter *after* I had already finished writing this section.
"Jesus is a contagious source of holiness that purges all manner of impurities
on contact. Therefore, his contact with death and subsequent resurrection en-
capsulates the salvation of the world, brought through the curse of death and
into indestructible life." Rillera, *Lamb of the Free*, 427.

begin to imagine our living, loving actions as a fragrant offering to God. Actions such as giving gifts to those in need, which is something Paul thanks the Philippians for doing.

> I have received full payment, and more. I am well supplied, having received from Epaphroditus the gifts you sent, a fragrant offering, a sacrifice acceptable and pleasing to God. (Phil 4:18 ESV)

Nine: What Does a Hand on the Head Do?

I HAD BETTER GIVE you the heads up: this section is going to be very Bible heavy. Here is the question we're trying to get our heads around: What does a hand on the head signify? There are many theories around, and no doubt you have your own. However, humour me for a moment—clear the table, put everything back in the kitchen drawer, and let's only put things back on the table as we find them in the Bible. To begin this challenge I've included a bit of a lengthy quote from the first chapter of Leviticus in the hope that we can get a feel for what happens after a hand touches a head. Don't take that fork out of the drawer yet, just read the text and try to grasp the flow of what is happening.

> Let him offer a male without blemish; he shall offer it of his own free will at the door of the tabernacle of meeting before the LORD. Then he shall put his hand on the head of the burnt offering, and it will be accepted on his behalf to make atonement for him. He shall kill the bull before the LORD; and the priests, Aaron's sons, shall bring the blood and sprinkle the blood all around on the altar that is by the door of the tabernacle of meeting. . . . Then the priests, Aaron's sons, shall lay the parts, the head, and the fat in order on the wood that is on the fire upon the altar; but he shall wash its entrails and its legs with water. And the priest shall burn all on the altar as a burnt sacrifice, an offering made by fire, a sweet aroma to the LORD. (Lev 1:3–9 NKJV)

The first thing that strikes me is the absence of any explanation around what a hand on the head might mean; we are just not told. However, here are some other things I notice. I notice that the animal is without blemish (wait for the next chapter). I notice the offerer offers "of his own free will"; there is no obligation or coercion. I notice that after the hand gesture everything including the head is received by God as a "sweet aroma." I notice that the entrails and legs are washed before being burned, but the head is not washed. I notice that after a hand is placed on the animal's head its blood is sprinkled all over the altar.

One of my personal preconceptions, perhaps a spoon that we just cleared off the table, was that a hand on the head transferred the offerer's sin to the animal. But does anything we've read so far allow us to put that spoon back on the table yet? If the animal had just received a dose of sin to the head, then we might imagine the animal would now be contaminated. Strange then that Yahweh considers that contaminated meat "a sweet aroma."

Perhaps the sin was directly transferred to the animal's head, but the rest of the body remained pure? Why then are the entrails and feet washed first, but the head goes straight onto the altar with the meat? Should we even put "sin" on the table just yet? The word *sin* doesn't show up till chapter 4 of Leviticus, so that spoon has to stay in the drawer for now.

Now, before we attempt to answer any more questions, I'm taking us outside Leviticus. Not too far out, only the next book: Numbers. Numbers is almost as fun as Leviticus, but just to make it slightly more fun I've removed some words.

> The Levites shall lay their hands on the heads of the young bulls, and you shall offer one as a sin offering and

the other as a burnt offering to the LORD. (Num 8:12
NKJV)

Let's compare that verse with the preceding verses—What do
you imagine they might be about?

> The children of Israel shall lay their hands on the _____
> and Aaron shall offer the _____ before the LORD like a
> wave offering. (Num 8:10–11 NKJV)

Ready for the big reveal? Here are those verses in their en-
tirety without any redactions:

> So you shall bring the Levites before the LORD, and the
> children of Israel shall lay their hands on the Levites; and
> Aaron shall offer the Levites before the LORD like a wave
> offering from the children of Israel, that they may per-
> form the work of the LORD. (Num 8:10–11 NKJV)

The choice to use almost identical language to describe both
Levites and animals as offerings to the LORD is surely supposed to
make us see them as somehow synonymous. Whatever a hand on
the head of a Levite means should help us understand what a hand
on an animal's head signifies. Notice what happens to the Levites
after hands are laid on them: just like the animal, they are presented
as an offering to Yahweh, for the special purpose of performing the
work of the LORD. Perhaps a hand on the head conveys consecration? Or designates a dedication for a special purpose?

If we want to put sin on the table, or sin on an animal's head,
we need to check how much the Bible has to say about it. Perhaps
it's only the sin offering that has sin transferred to it? What about
the other four offerings, did they also receive a dose of sin to the
head? Remember how shocked we were to discover that the word
sacrifice doesn't show up till chapter 3 of Leviticus? Well, a quick
concordance check shows that the word *sin* doesn't show up in
Leviticus until chapter 4! By which time we've already read about
three other offerings. When we do finally get an offering for sin,
it does indeed receive a hand on the head, but so have the burnt
and the peace offerings. Interestingly (and a little confoundingly),
there is no hand on the head mentioned for the guilt offering (nor,

obviously, the grain offering) and yet atonement and forgiveness are still offered: "The priest shall make atonement for him concerning his sin which he committed unintentionally and did not know it, and it will be forgiven him. It is a guilt offering" (Lev 5:18–19 NASB).

In this next chunk from Leviticus we'll see the word *sin*, and so we should pause and consider if that spoon should finally come out of the drawer.

> Then he brought the bull of the sin offering, and Aaron and his sons laid their hands on the head of the bull of the sin offering. Next Moses slaughtered it and took the blood and with his finger put some of it around on the horns of the altar, and purified the altar. Then he poured out the rest of the blood at the base of the altar and consecrated it. (Lev 8:14–15 NASB)

Linguistically it makes little sense that sin would be transferred to the bull and immediately blood from this sin-covered bull would be considered an appropriate substance to pour over the altar. How could blood from a sin-covered animal consecrate anything?

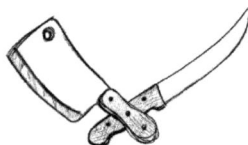

So far we've seen that a hand can be placed on an animal or a human. The blood from that animal is used to cleanse and to purify. The animal is considered suitable to be given to God on his holy altar. The smell of that offering is pleasant to God. And when it is a human who has received a hand on the head they enter into a life of holy service to God. As the Levites receive a hand on the head and their life is transformed from an ordinary life into one of holy service doing God's work, perhaps the animal is transformed from a common animal into one that enters into holy space? Staying in chapter 8 of Leviticus, let's continue on and notice what else occurs after a hand has been placed on a head.

> Then he presented the second ram, the ram of ordina-tion, and Aaron and his sons laid their hands on the head of the ram. And Moses slaughtered it and took some of its blood and put it on the lobe of Aaron's right ear, and on the thumb of his right hand and on the big toe of his right foot. . . . Then Moses said to Aaron and to his sons, "Boil the flesh at the doorway of the tent of meeting, and eat it there together with the bread which is in the basket of the ordination offering, just as I commanded, saying, 'Aaron and his sons shall eat it.'" (Lev 8:22–23, 31 NASB)

Aaron and his sons lay a hand on the head of a ram, and its blood is applied to their ears, thumbs, and big toes. Again to con-secrate them. And then they sit down to a meal. And what are they eating? The meat from the ram. If sin had just been transferred onto this animal, surely we would not expect sin-contaminated meat to be eaten by holy priests? Some scholars have even suggested that placing your hand on the animal shows that you are identifying with the animal, or that the animal is "taking your place." However this doesn't make much sense as this animal is being eaten by the people who placed their hand on its head. Would you select an animal with which you are identifying, seeing this animal as your representative, and then would you cook it and eat it? You would be symbolically eating yourself.

I know you love Leviticus, and you've read about the scape-goat. And so I know you're probably yelling at me, "Phil, there is an animal that has sin placed on its head." Yes, you are correct. And this animal only reinforces what I've been saying. I'm not even kidding.

This goat does receive a hand on its head. "Aaron will lay both his hands on the head of the live goat . . . —all their sins. He is to put them on the goat's head" (Lev 16:21 CSB). It then becomes increasingly apparent that this goat is most definitely a sin-contaminated creature. And so this animal doesn't get eaten. It is not offered to God. It would most certainly not give off a pleas-ing aroma. Its blood isn't used for cleansing. In fact, if you've been reading through Leviticus, and you've become familiar with the rhythm of the rituals, you will turn to chapter 16 and notice a jar-ring change in the language. You would notice that for the first time the priest places *two* hands on the head of this animal instead of one. You will read quite explicitly that all the sin of the Israelites is put on the head of this poor goat. This is, in fact, the first and only time in the entire Bible where we read about an animal being burdened with sin.

We further see how defiled this goat must have been when we read that the man who leads the goat into the wilderness has to wash and change his clothes before he can come back into the camp. And that is another major difference. The only animal that is expressly said to have sin placed on its head is led away and not killed. Importantly the defiled goat is led *away* from God, the opposite of drawing near.

At this point you may be asking a very valid question. Why did the scapegoat handler have to wash his clothes and bathe his body after handling this goat, but there was no washing requirement for any of the other offerings? The answer is precisely because this goat was most contaminated with sin, while the other offerings remained pure.

Apart from this one poor goat who carries the sin away, the Bible never uses the language of "bearing sin" to describe animals. There are other "sin bearers" in the Bible, but they're not animals. It may surprise you to learn that the only other sin bearers are Yahweh himself (Exod 34:7; Ps 25:18), priests (Exod 28:38; Lev 10:17), and the Isaiah servant (Isa 53:12)—but that's a topic for another book.

Leaving the live goat alone to wander for now, I tried to see if any early church fathers had anything to say on the subject of hand-laying, but intriguingly there was almost nothing to be found, and this in itself is telling. More recent commentary has *loads* to say on the subject. This is also telling, not least because these recent (post-Reformation) interpretations are also overwhelmingly contradictory.

Philo of Alexandria was a Jewish philosopher and writer born around 10 BC, who wrote copious volumes on the Hebrew Bible and the Jewish sacrificial system. He has an intriguing theory.

> The hands which are laid upon the head of the animal are
> a most manifest symbol of irreproachable actions, and of
> a life which does nothing which is open to accusation.[1]

The symbolic action, as Philo sees it, is basically a demonstration that the person bringing the offering came free of guilt. Philo, a Jew, living at a time when sacrifices were a daily occurrence, surely holds more authority on the subject than most post-Reformation speculations.

However, one of the most helpful books I read while researching Leviticus was a very recent book by Abby Kaplan called *Misreading Ritual: Sacrifice and Purity for the Modern-Day Gentile.* I read pretty much everything I could lay my hands on on this subject, but Kaplan recounted a theory that stood out to me as especially compelling.[2] She recounts a theory popularised by Jacob Milgrom,[3] that the hand-leaning gesture demonstrates who is bringing the offering. It signifies to God, *this offering is from my hand.* And the suggestion is that this is why a hand on the head is not required for birds—because when a person carries a bird in their hands it is obvious who has brought the offering. Simply, scholars suggest that laying one hand on the head of an animal identifies the offerer as its owner. (And this may go quite a way to explain why the priest lays two hands on the goat, if the goat that is sent away is for the whole of the Israelite community.)

1. Philo, "Special Laws," 202.

2. Kaplan, *Misreading Ritual*, 77.

3. Jacob Milgrom popularised this theory, and others agree, including Andrew Remington Rillera.

This next story, however, really threw a spanner in the works.

> The son of the Israelite woman blasphemed the Name
> and cursed. So they brought him to Moses. . . . Then
> Yahweh spoke to Moses, saying, "Bring the one who has
> cursed outside the camp, and let all who heard him lay
> their hands on his head; then let all the congregation
> stone him." (Lev 24:11–14)

This really threw me when I first read it. A man has been heard blaspheming the name of Yahweh, and he has been condemned to death. So one thing is obvious: the Israelites who lay their hands on him are not transferring their sin to this man—he is already guilty. Perhaps this confirms Philo's theory that the people attached to the hands are free of guilt? Maybe these hands are confirming the offender's guilt? Likewise, if hands on an animal show it becoming guilty and deserving death, we may have solved the puzzle. However this theory most definitely does *not* work for the Levites or the priests, who are neither guilty nor condemned, but rather are cleansed and consecrated. Here we may think of the scapegoat, an animal bearing guilt and deserving death. That is, until we remember that this goat doesn't actually get killed. Could we see this blaspheming man as being presented "on behalf of" or "in the place of" the Israelite witnesses? No, he is not dying as a substitute; he is definitely dying for his own crime.

A guilty blasphemer, innocent Levites, unblemished animals, a sin-covered goat, purified priests—they all experience a hand on their head. But is there a unifying theme to tie them all together?

Unfortunately, I don't believe the Bible allows us to arrive at a definitive conclusion. All that cutlery will have to stay in the drawer, and that's okay. Should we throw our hands up in exasperation? There's loads more to explore; we haven't even considered Joseph's sons (Gen 48:14), or Joshua (Deut 34:9; Num 27:18–19). There is someone else we could turn to for help . . . But before we ask him, something we read right back at the beginning of Leviticus may in fact be the closest we are going to get to an answer from any single verse in the Bible.

> And he shall lay his hand on the head of the burnt offering, so that it may be accepted for him to make atonement on his behalf. (Lev 1:4 NASB)

While we're not told the *how*, we are told the *why*. Apparently the outcome is important, even if we are not provided with an explanation for how the mechanism operates.

It does occur to me that there is someone else we could turn to for help. His name is Jesus, and if "Christ our Passover lamb has been sacrificed" (1 Cor 5:7 CSB), then maybe he had a hand placed on his head?[4] The gospel writers go to a lot of effort to demonstrate Jesus as fulfilling all the important tropes of the Hebrew sacrificial and priestly roles. So might we expect them to include a helpful

---

4. Even though the Passover lamb did not actually receive a hand on the head.

hand on the head to provide a hint as to the elusive meaning behind this gesture?

Perhaps Matthew mentions a hand on Jesus' head before he began his ministry, demonstrating dedication or consecration? A strategically placed hand on the head at Jesus' trial could illustrate his innocence, or his alleged guilt? When Jesus was baptised by John in the Jordan River, did part of John's baptism ceremony involve laying a hand on Jesus' head? It's certainly possible, perhaps even likely; it definitely would have been a helpful detail to include, but for some reason the gospel writers in their wisdom chose to leave out this detail. The woman who touched the hem of Jesus' garment, might she not have *laid a hand on him*? Might not Jesus have felt her illness or her sin transferred to him? But that's not how the gospel writers portray what happened. A discreet hand on Jesus' head before his death might solve our dilemma. Why didn't the gospel writers implement Leviticus language when describing the crown of thorns placed on Jesus' head? When Jesus was *slapped* and *hit*, Luke could have cleverly recounted the event as *they laid their hands on him and hit him*. Was this a missed opportunity? Or was a hand on the head just not a necessary way to communicate Jesus' embodiment of a sacrificial ritual?

Alas, as far as I could find, Jesus never had a hand placed on his head. One thing I'm realising, and this may be where I land, is that if it was not important for the gospel writers to present Jesus as having a hand on his head, then perhaps I need to keep that particular kitchen drawer closed. Whatever hands on heads signifies, perhaps it communicates nothing necessary for how we understand Jesus' sacrifice.

Ten: What Does an Unblemished Life Look Like?

AT ONE TIME IT wasn't uncommon for me to walk into the cool room and punch a lamb. I mean, a lamb hanging upside down on a hook does look like an inviting punching bag. If I punched hard enough, I would break a rib. If I punched really hard, I could break several ribs. But a broken bone rendered an animal unacceptable for God's table. One implicit teaching from this is that the animals were not to be treated harshly. They were not to be beaten. Nor were they spat on, mocked, or tortured. Instead, only the best, faultless, closest to perfect animals could be given to Yahweh. The word Leviticus uses to describe this state is *unblemished*.

One day as part of my training as an apprentice, we went on an excursion to the abattoir, and it so happened that it was Jewish kosher day. One thing I have never forgotten is how the man performing the slaughter, known as a shochet, ran his fingernail along the length of the blade between each slaughter. If he found a nick or a slight imperfection in the blade, out came his sharpening stone, and he rubbed the blade back to a perfect edge. This is mainly to ensure the slaughter is as quick and painless as possible. But if the animal is killed with an imperfect knife, it is no longer considered kosher. Basically, a blemish in the knife renders the animal unacceptable.

Previously I mentioned that when slicing up steaks you can easily tell if the animal had been bruised while it was alive. Bruised meat does not look very appetising, and so the bruise is usually trimmed off and discarded. It goes without saying that God doesn't like bruised animals either. Damaged or bruised animals were considered *blemished*, and could not be offered to Yahweh.

> You are not to present to the LORD an animal whose testicles are bruised, crushed, torn, or cut; you are not to sacrifice them in your land. Neither you nor a foreigner shall present food to your God from any such animal. They will not be accepted on your behalf, because they are deformed and flawed. (Lev 22:24–25 BSB)

To fully understand what an unblemished animal looks like, we first need to understand what a *blemished* animal looks like, and *deformed* and *flawed* are good words to start with. Fortunately for us, Leviticus supplies a list of all things that make an animal unacceptable.

> It must be without defect to be accepted; there shall be no defect in it. Those that are blind, fractured, maimed, or have a wart, a festering rash, or scabs, you shall not offer to the LORD, nor make of them an offering by fire on the altar to the LORD. (Lev 22:21–22 NASB)

The English word *blemish* is not a bad translation, but it falls short of providing the full picture, because in Hebrew a *blemished* animal means it is no longer complete. It has something missing or something out of place, like a missing eye, or a wart. And this helps reveal what the word *unblemished* is trying to communicate: *complete*. An unblemished animal is whole and complete, lacking nothing, nothing out of place.

Okay, time out. Dearest reader, we need to have a little chat. I've been using the word *unblemished*, but you may be aware that some translations use the

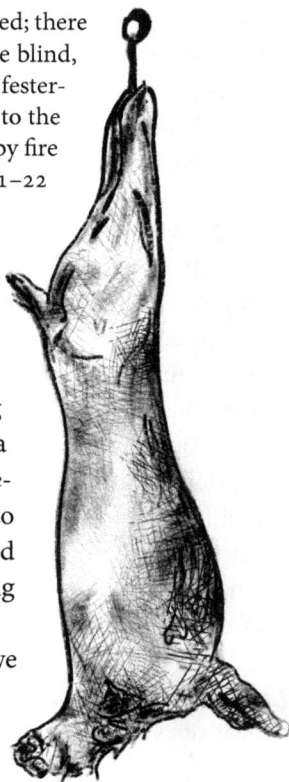

word *blameless*. I'm intentionally avoiding this word because I don't like it. And I don't like it for a pastoral reason. If an animal is born blind, it is no longer blameless. If a lamb is attacked by a wolf and limps away with a broken foot, it is no longer blameless. Should the lamb have run faster? Was it the lamb's fault? You see, the word *blameless* contains the word *blame*. Suggesting that an animal is only free of blame, blame-*less*, if it doesn't have a deformity is one thing. But throughout the Bible humans are also exhorted to be blameless. Abram is told to "walk before me and be blameless" (Gen 17:1), and there is a recurring theme that the blameless will be blessed by Yahweh (Ps 37:18; Ps 119:1; Prov 28:18).

And so, as a human, if you are no longer blame-*less*, what are you? I looked up antonyms for the word *blameless*, and found words like *blameworthy, condemned, shamed, punishable, accused, at fault*. Unfortunately, the choice to use a word that contains blame may give the impression that, if I have a deformity, I am at fault. Should I be blamed for being born with a disability? Does a baby born blind deserve punishment? Is someone with cancer culpable? Should I be punished for my mental illness?

Happily, the Hebrew has nothing to do with blame. There is no notion of guilt or shame contained in the word, and so obviously animals are not held responsible for their deformity. In one place Leviticus says, "You are to count seven *complete* weeks" (Lev 23:15 CSB, emphasis added). Other translations say "count off seven *full* weeks" (NIV, emphasis added) or "seven *perfect* sabbaths" (YLT,[1] emphasis added). It's the same word, *blameless*, but here we see what the word really means: perfect. Not in the sense of morally perfect, but more like *entirely whole and complete*. In English we might say "We were perfect strangers" or "I felt like a perfect idiot," meaning *complete strangers*, or a *complete idiot*.

An animal that is *blemished* is incomplete—it is no longer whole, no longer in its *intended state*. And if we know anything by now, we should realise that giving something to God that is outside

---

1. Scripture quotations marked (YLT) are taken from the 1898 *Young's Literal Translation of the Holy Bible* by J. N. Young. This version of the Bible is in the public domain.

its intended state is not such a sharp idea. Offering these types of animals to God is seen as a slap in the face, and, indeed, God takes it personally. In fact, he has a serious beef with certain priests who are defiling and profaning his holy name, as the prophet Malachi records.

> Priests who despise My name! But you say, "How have we despised Your name?" You are presenting defiled food upon My altar. But you say, "How have we defiled You?" In that you say, "The table of the LORD is to be despised." And when you present a blind animal for sacrifice, is it not evil? Or when you present a lame or sick animal, is it not evil? (Mal 1:6–8 NASB)

Here we get a glimpse as to why these kinds of offerings would be outrageously unacceptable and, moreover, why presenting such an inadequate gift is described as *evil*. Yahweh goes on to say, "Try offering them to your governor! Would he be pleased with you? Would he accept you?" (v. 8 NIV).

If you were invited out on a romantic date night, and you turned up with flowers but they were drooping and dying, would you be accepted? Would your date be pleased with you? What about if you worked at a winery, and you had access to a selection of truly amazing wines but, instead of bringing one of the best bottles, you brought a cheap bottle that had been rolling around the floor of your car for a week? When viewed this way, the gift can be understood as a representation of the offerer's heart. The gift reflects the intention of the giver. And this begins to explain why Yahweh desires only unblemished animals.

Intriguingly, when describing an unblemished animal, we are not given any moral requirements. The Israelites are not required to check the animal's personality or check for character flaws. One reason is this: unlike a devious human heart, an animal with no physical defect is much easier to discern. In other words, an unblemished animal was supposed to be a tangible image of the offerer's hidden heart. Here's our friend Philo again.

> Accordingly, the man who is about to offer a sacrifice ought to examine and see, not whether the animal is

without blemish, but whether his mind is sound, and entire, and perfect.[2]

Remember the list of things that rendered an animal blemished: any animal with an impairment—blind, fractured, maimed, warts, festering rash, scabs, crushed testicles (Lev 22). Well, flip back a page in your Bible and compare that list to what makes a priest unable to draw near . . .

> No man who has any defect may come near: no man who is blind or lame, disfigured or deformed; no man with a crippled foot or hand, or who is a hunchback or a dwarf, or who has any eye defect, or who has festering or running sores or damaged testicles. No descendant of Aaron the priest who has any defect is to come near to present the food offerings to the LORD. (Lev 21:18–21 NIV)

Previously we noted the similarities between placing a hand on an animal as an offering to Yahweh and placing a hand on the Levites before they entered into work for Yahweh. And now we might wonder what unblemished animals have in common with priests? The physical requirements for priests to be able to draw near and handle holy things mirrors almost exactly the physical requirements for an animal offering to be placed on Yahweh's altar. And doesn't it all seem a bit . . . discriminatory? Intolerant?

It's one thing that an animal must have no defect to be accepted, but a priest? Any Levite born blind, anyone with a skin blemish, anyone who limps is rejected by God because apparently his holiness can't tolerate deformity. I mean, really, surely moral integrity should be God's benchmark; surely man looks at outward appearances but God looks at the heart. This sounds to my ears

2. Philo, "Special Laws," 283.

like a God who discriminates and who excludes anyone with a disability. Yes. It does. And it's not an unfair criticism. You may have heard people say things like "God's holiness requires perfection," "You cannot approach God in your sinful state," or "There is an unsurpassable chasm between you and God."

Let me ask you a question. What does an unblemished animal entering holy space teach us about God's character? One way to answer that question would be: no one may draw near to God *unless* they are perfect. Another way to answer the question could be: God *desires* a complete life without blemish to dwell with him in his holy presence. God wants to live in the midst of humanity. He is extending an invitation back into the garden space, and there is a dress code. The priests and the animals are like models on a catwalk, demonstrating not who we *must* be but who we *will* be. The unblemished priests parade as God's representatives, the animals without defect present an image of the "sound, entire, and perfect" mind that we will possess when we, too, are drawn into God's presence. God is showing us the clothes we will be given, the healed and whole state of our liver and kidneys—no deception in our passions, no wound in our emotions. We will be free from defect. We will be made whole and complete: no more cancer, no more broken bones, no blindness, no debilitating disease.[3]

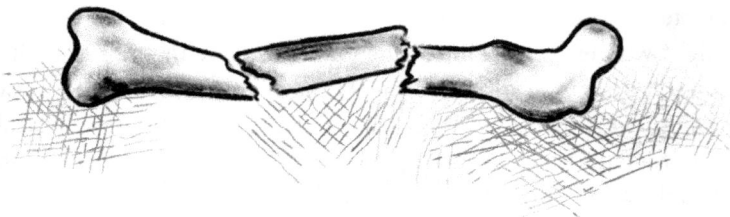

3. An alternate view, and a thought experiment worth pondering, is presented in the book *Perfect in Weakness*, where the author wonders, since Christ's resurrected body retained his scars, perhaps those who consider their "unique embodiment" to be identity forming, whether physical or mental, might retain that characteristic as an essential and good part of their resurrected body. See Whitaker, *Perfect in Weakness*.

Perhaps your *blemish* isn't physical. Perhaps it's your mind. Your mental health. Maybe your morals are compromised. Perhaps you were the child that had an absent or abusive parent, and grew up unable to experience complete safety, never knowing full love. There may be parts of your personality that aren't fully developed; you may even have developed your own moral blindness.

Or perhaps you are the mother who was too unwell to care for her newborn baby, and you feel like you have a gaping hole in your own life and worry you have left a gaping hole in your child's life.

My dearest reader, rest assured, God's desire is to dwell with you in the midst of that guilt and pain, and as he sits with you he is saying, "I want to make you whole again." And deep within, you know this to be true because you can imagine the daily spectacle of seeing perfect, complete animals enter into God's holy space. And every one of them is accepted by God. You know that God is showing you what life is like in his presence: No guilt. No depression. No anxiety. No failures. No faults.

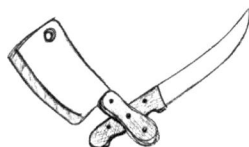

> LORD, who may dwell in your sacred tent?
> Who may live on your holy mountain?
> The one whose walk is blameless. (Ps 15:1–2 NIV)

Complete weeks, perfect priests, entirely sound animals, but what does a blameless *walk* look like? What would a complete human look like? Has there ever been a human whose walk was complete, who lived a complete life? Did Adam and Eve experience completeness before they fell out of God's intended order? It seems the psalmist assumes that all those who dwell in Yahweh's presence will be complete. Perhaps he is eagerly looking forward to the day when he is living in Yahweh's house, sharing an intimate relationship with the Father, lacking nothing, complete in every way.

How might someone become complete?

> For in Christ all the fullness of the Deity dwells in bodily form. And you have been made complete in Christ. (Col 2:9–10 BSB)

There you have it. Jesus lived an unblemished life; he is in fact called "a lamb without blemish or defect" (1 Pet 1:19 NIV). What does a complete human look like? Jesus. How do we become complete? I would suggest it is impossible to be a complete human apart from Christ and his body. It is only in Christ that we are complete; apart from him we can do nothing (John 15:5). It is only as we participate in him, united with him as his body—the body of Christ—that we will experience what it is to be a complete human.

Being able to draw near and dwell in Yahweh's tent is extraordinary, but something else has extraordinarily changed as a result of Jesus' unblemished actions.

One thing we've learnt from Leviticus is that Yahweh does not reside in impure spaces. So when God says, "I will put my Spirit within you" (Ezek 36:27), and that *the Spirit of God dwells in us* (Eph 2:20–22; Rom 8:9, 11, 15), it can only be because humanity has been cleansed and made holy. Something radical must have happened for our infinitely holy God to take up residence in humanity. Something for which the tent, and sacrifice, and the purity laws, and Leviticus have all been forward-pointing signposts. Because today we participate in that reality, together, as Christ's body: a dwelling place on earth for the spirit of God.

> Do you not know that you are a temple of God and that the Spirit of God dwells in you? (1 Cor 3:16 NASB)

As we live a united life, knowing that Jesus in his mercy has united humanity to himself, the actions of his body are *acceptable* to God. Our life is acceptable, our actions become a sweet smelling aroma, precisely because we are acting as the body of Christ. Paul describes the body of Christ as "a glorious church, not having spot, or wrinkle, . . . holy and without blemish" (Eph 5:27 KJV).

And of this body, Christ is the head, and we are parts—members of Christ's body. He is seated enthroned in the heavens, and we are seated with him (Eph 2:6), although we still struggle in the mud as his feet, and strive as his hands in the dirt, yet we are being steadily transformed, through the sanctifying work of the Holy Spirit.

Eleven: How Is Splattering Blood Considered Clean?

EARLY ON AS AN apprentice, while I was working sixty-hour weeks in a butcher shop, most of my friends were still at school or university. So I looked forward to every Friday night, when we could catch up at church youth group. One day while at work I thought it would be funny or clever or something to put some real blood of a lamb on my Bible. I smeared it over the inside cover of the book. Then, of course, I brought the Bible to youth group to show off my creative wit. I remember someone, a girl I liked, asking "What's that?" and I said with a clever smirk, "That's the blood of the lamb," and she said, "That's disgusting Phil." I didn't have a girlfriend for a while . . .

For us today, blood is a little bit disgusting (unless you're a juvenile butcher). But for ancient people blood was viewed very differently. For ancient people blood held highly potent properties.

> Anyone from the house of Israel, or from the strangers who reside among them, who eats any blood, I will set My face against that person who eats the blood. (Lev 17:10 NASB)

Why the adverse reaction to blood? Why would God's posture be wrath towards some poor person who ate black pudding for breakfast? In the previous chapter we noticed a dilemma: death couldn't come into contact with God's holy altar, but somehow splashing blood around was okay. This is because blood is not associated with death. Blood is in fact life.

> But you shall not eat flesh with its life, that is, its blood.
> (Gen 9:4 NASB)

Some translations refer to it as *lifeblood*, which is a translation choice I particularly like as it succinctly communicates this ancient blood-equals-life paradigm. After the warning to not consume blood in chapter 17, just in case you hadn't quite got the message yet, Leviticus reiterates the point. Four times.

> For the life of the flesh is in the blood . . . for it is the blood by reason of the life that makes atonement. . . . For as for the life of all flesh, its blood is identified with its life. . . . The life of all flesh is its blood. (Lev 17:11, 14 NASB)

And so when we read about blood being splashed around in a sacrificial or ceremonial context we are to imagine lashings of *life* being thrown about. Remember how my boning knife removes bones, and how Moses *sinned* the altar, removing the sin? What did Moses use to remove the sin? You guessed it: blood.

> Moses slaughtered the bull and took some of the blood, and with his finger he put it on all the horns of the altar to purify the altar. He poured out the rest of the blood at the base of the altar. So he consecrated it to make atonement for it. (Lev 8:15 NIV)

Blood—lifeblood—is the ancient equivalent of a spray bottle of cleaning fluid. Moses is effectively taking aim with his bottle of lifeblood, and disinfecting the altar. Lifeblood purifies or removes all the Israelite sin that had spread and contaminated the altar. Remember all the things that were considered unclean, all those things outside God's created order: body fluids on the outside, sea creatures that creep onto the dry land. Well . . . surely *sin* is outside of God's intended order. And just as *sin* sits outside God's good order, so does *death*. And here we begin to see God's answer to the problem of sin and death. Life.

As blood is synonymous with life, now *lifeblood* can be seen as the antidote to death.

Throughout Leviticus blood is applied to many different surfaces: the horns of the altar, the mercy seat, a priest's earlobe, even poured out on the ground. In the butcher shop when someone drops a piece of meat onto the ground, without fail, someone will yell out, "Did you want that freshly ground?" The reason for pouring the blood onto the ground is not explicitly obvious. It could be to eliminate any temptation a priest may have to consume life. It could be providing an appropriate burial, so to speak, for the *life* of the animal. It could be giving the *life* back to the dust from where life came (Gen 3:19).

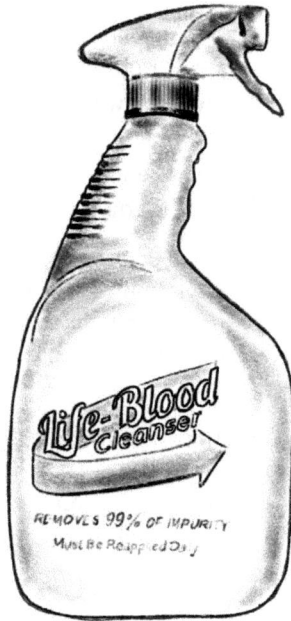

When lifeblood is applied to objects like the altar, however, life is being liberally applied in a place that has been contaminated by impurity, sin, and death. Moses, spray bottle in hand, is sanitising the infected areas. Whatever has happened in the Israelite camp—sin, death, mould, sickness, a dodgy real estate deal, a hateful heart—all this impurity has spread like an invisible vapour throughout the Israelite camp, contaminating everything; it may have even seeped inside the tent and contaminated holy space. We see Aaron dealing with this threat of contamination on the Day of Atonement: "With his finger he shall sprinkle some of the blood on it [the altar] seven times and cleanse it, and consecrate it from the impurities of the sons of Israel" (Lev 16:19 NASB).

The altar and the atonement cover; these objects aren't to be held morally culpable, yet they are still affected by sin. Just by sitting there, quietly minding their own business, they have become contaminated. What about a living person recovering from a disease like leprosy? The prescription for a sick human is the same as for an infected object: "The priest shall then take some of the blood of the guilt offering, and the priest shall put it on the lobe of the right ear of the one to be cleansed" (Lev 14:14). Whether it is a piece of furniture in Yahweh's throne room, or a man recovering from leprosy, the solution is the same: cleansing is performed by administering lifeblood.

In chapter 4 we learned that a *nearness gift* is the thing that is *brought near*. In Lev 1:5 that same word is used about the blood: "The priests shall *bring near* the blood" (Lev 1:5). And on the Day of Atonement, lifeblood actually comes closer to Yahweh's presence than anything or anyone else, closer even than a human. In Lev 16:15 the blood of an animal is sprinkled over the mercy seat, the very place where Yahweh's presence appears and is most concentrated. If you think about it, this means an unblemished *life* is sharing the same space as God's intense presence. An unblemished life is able to enter into Yahweh's presence and encounter his glory. I think this is pointing to the hope for humanity; an ideal human, God's complete image, who, living an unblemished life, is able to draw near to Yahweh, to go all the way in, to exist in his presence, share in his glory, and dwell with him in his house.

Through lifeblood, God is revealing his plan to make creation complete, to renew it, to remove all the sin, all the impurity, all the death, to put everything back in its intended order. There is a problem, however; animal blood deals with the effects of impurities but not the source. It's like when I spray sanitiser onto my bench. It cleans the contaminated surface, but it doesn't address how the contamination got there in the first place.[1] The implicit hope, therefore, must be for something more substantial than animal blood. Because animal blood has an inherent problem: it has to be reapplied repeatedly. Animal blood doesn't seem to keep a thing clean forever. The reason for this is probably because animals are mortal. Animals still die. And so their blood is not immune to death. Perhaps what we need is an immortal animal? If only there was some way we could get our hands on the blood of an unblemished eternal being. If only an eternal being would share his lifeblood with us.

"The life is in the blood." Does Jesus affirm those words? Not only does he affirm those words, he identifies himself as the source of that life and he offers that life to us: "Unless you eat the flesh of the Son of Man and drink His blood, you have no life in you" (John 6:53 NKJV).

> Then he took a cup, and when he had given thanks, he gave it to them, saying, "Drink from it, all of you. This is my blood." (Matt 26:27–28 NIV)

I don't know about you, but sometimes I really feel like I need to do something physical to help *feel* cleansed and forgiven. Sometimes not even because I've done something especially sinful but because I feel the grime of living in a greasy and stained world. And yet I do sin. And I feel like I need a regular physical reminder that Jesus has taken care of it all. I feel a need to drink the wine— the cleansing blood of Jesus. I long to experience an assurance that

---

1. Matthew Thiessen unpacks this in his 2020 book *Jesus and the Forces of Death: The Gospels' Portrayal of Ritual Impurity Within First-Century Judaism.*

even though the world I live in is messy, even though I sin, as the wine fills my insides, I am being cleansed from my insides out.

And then I remember that "the *life* is in the blood." Whose life are we receiving when we drink the cup? God is filling us, purifying us, removing sin, cleansing impurity, filling a contaminated vessel with his life.

Twelve: Can Atonement Really Remove Sin?

2500 BC, ANCIENT SYRIA, a stone tablet contains an inscription describing the preparations for a royal wedding, and how the house of the dead must first be purified.[1] The tablet describes a live goat being sent out and released, carrying with it any impurity, thus allowing the gods, and the king and queen, to enter the mausoleum as part of the wedding ceremony.

> We purify the mausoleum before the entrance of the gods Kura and Barama. A goat, a silver bracelet hanging from its neck, towards the steppe of Alini we let it go.

Late Bronze age, Hattusa—the capital of the Hittite Empire—a ceremony for the purification of the king and queen:

> The exorcist releases one bull for the king, and one cow, ewe, and nanny goat for the queen's implements—all as a *nakušši* (sent-away)—and then declares as follows:
> "Whatever evil word, false oath, curse, or impurity has been committed in the sight of the deity—may these *nakuššis* carry them off from before the deity. May the deity and the king and queen be purified of these things!"

Close by, another ancient Hittite ritual describes how evil is removed from a sick or afflicted person; it is transferred to a mouse via a red thread, and the mouse is sent away and released in an

---

1. Ayali-Darshan, "Scapegoat Ritual." In the ancient rituals described here, I've slightly paraphrased the quotes to make them easier to read. The full article is amazing, and worth reading in full.

uninhabited region as a gift for the gods Zarniza and Tarpattašši who reside there.

> She [the exorcist] wraps a small piece of tin in a thread and binds it around the right hand and foot of the afflicted person. Then she takes it from them, binding it around a mouse: "I have taken the evil from you. I have bound it around the mouse. May this mouse carry it to the high mountains, to the deepest valleys, to the long roads."
>
> Then they release the mouse: "Zarniza, Tarpattašši— You, take this for yourself, and we shall give you something else to eat."

1400 BC, the port city of Ugarit—a trading partner with Egypt and the Hittite Empire—the following instructions are found:

> If a city is captured or if the people die, all the people shall take a goat and lead it far off.

800 BC, at the height of the Neo-Assyrian Empire, a stone tablet describes a ritual for removing evil and disease from a sick person. The sick person spits into a frog's mouth, symbolically passing the illness into it, a red and white thread is attached to its feet, tied on with thorns, and the live frog is taken back to the water where it is released. The following words are spoken:

> Frog, you know the disease which seized me. . . . When you hop off and return to your waters, you will return the evil to its steppe.

Early Iron Age, a scroll containing priestly instructions for cleansing a Hebrew house that has been contaminated with mould. The priest takes two clean birds, slaughters one and collects its blood. He takes cedar wood, hyssop, and a red thread and dips them in the blood, along with the second, live bird. The live bird is then released to fly away over an open field.

> He shall let the live bird go free outside the city into the open field. So he shall make atonement for the house, and it will be clean. (Lev 14:53)

That last story is from, you guessed it, Leviticus. The ritual of the two birds is somewhat of a parallel to another ritual I'm sure you're familiar with: the Day of Atonement. Once you notice those similarities sitting alongside the other rituals performed by Israel's neighbours, it provides an indispensable cultural lens through which to understand what the two goats are doing on the Day of Atonement.

All of those ancient rituals share a common action: some kind of uncleanness or evil is attached to a live animal that is sent away and released. Today they're often called *scapegoat* rituals, and that's a word we can thank Tyndale for. In 1530, when translating the Torah, Tyndale made up the word *scapegoat* because he saw a goat that *escapes* or an *escape goat*.

As you read through Leviticus, when you turn the page to chapter 16 and start reading about the Day of Atonement, you will notice a jarring change of language. Normally a section begins with the phrase "The LORD said to Moses," but chapter 16 begins with a double reference to God speaking (16:1–2a). Aaron is told to "bathe his body in water" before he changes into "holy garments," which are white priestly garments and a turban—different from his normal priestly attire. Then Aaron is instructed to take "two goats and set them before the LORD at the entrance of the tent of meeting. And Aaron shall cast lots over the two goats, one lot for the LORD and the other lot for Azazel" (Lev 16:7–8 ESV).

Two goats; this is new. Casting lots over the goats; this is unprecedented. One goat for Yahweh, one for someone called Azazel; this is scandalous. The outrageous drama continues as one goat is not killed but is instead released. This goat has two hands placed on its head instead of one. And then, something never seen anywhere else in the Bible: this goat has all the iniquities, transgressions, and sins of Israel placed on its head. This word *transgression* is also unique, occurring only twice in Leviticus, here, in chapter 16. Lastly, this goat is referred to three times as the "live goat." All of this is new. Something extraordinary is happening here.

So here we have a live goat, with a great big pile of sin on its head. What do you suppose should happen to this four-footed courier carrying all the sin and evil of thousands of people? Should it be punished? Beaten? Tortured? Killed? All other animal offerings in Leviticus are killed, so it may seem the expected next act in this drama. But, as I've said before, the *only* animal in the whole Bible that is expressly said to have sin placed on it is also the animal that is specifically *not* killed. Instead, this live goat is led away from Israel, outside the camp, taking all their impurities and uncleanness with it, where it is sent on its way. No blood, no torture, no death. And so, dear reader, if an Israelite was to observe an animal, carrying a load of sin, and that animal was led away, released, and not killed, what might this be teaching that Israelite about what Yahweh does with sin?

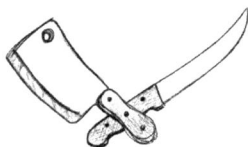

The Day of Atonement, or Yom Kippur, is still considered to be the most important festival on the Jewish calendar today. The English word *atonement* is another word we can thank Tyndale for. Basically, when he came to the Hebrew word *kippur*, he couldn't think of a suitable English word, so he made one up. He thought *kippur* contained the idea of being reconciled to God, or God and humanity being "at one," so he invented the word *at-one-ment*. Which is a great made-up word, until you realise that atonement is also made for houses, the tabernacle, and the altar, and, well, being *at one* with an altar doesn't sound very appealing.

The Hebrew root of *kippur* means "wipe," and depending on how it's used it can mean to wipe on, or wipe off, or wipe away. I've come to realise, however, that the full meaning of atonement cannot be reduced to one or two words, or even a made-up word. The full picture of atonement can only be understood within the drama of a whole *Day* of Atonement.

The drama unfolds as follows:

> Aaron shall lay both his hands on the head of the live
> goat, and confess over it all the iniquities of the people
> of Israel, and all their transgressions, all their sins. And
> he shall put them on the head of the goat and send it
> away into the wilderness by the hand of a man who is in
> readiness. The goat shall bear all their iniquities on itself
> to a remote area, and he shall let the goat go free in the
> wilderness. (Lev 16:21–22 ESV)

All Israel's sin is placed on the head of a live goat. But not simply their sin; Leviticus uses three different Hebrew words for sin: *iniquities, transgressions, sins.* I mentioned before that one of these words, *transgression*, only appears here in Lev 16 as it is placed on the head of this live goat. So whatever all the other offerings are doing—the guilt offering, the sin offering—they are not dealing with transgression. This annual cleanout is apparently the only way to completely cleanse the Israelite camp without leaving any trace of transgression. Scholars used to suggest that atonement meant to *cover*. But atonement cannot be about simply sweeping dirt under the carpet, or placing a rug over an ugly stain. Neither is this ritual about *forgive and forget*. In an ancient mind, transgressions, iniquities, and sin were real things that couldn't just be covered up and ignored. This is why atonement must mean so much more than merely covering over sin to hide it from God; sin had to be wiped away and removed.

Over the course of the year, all of Israel's sin, iniquity, and transgression had built up, covering the camp, contaminating the tent, and infecting the community. What's the best way to remove this sin contamination? Blood. Lifeblood.

The day begins with the high priest washing himself and changing into special garments. He then slowly advances towards Yahweh's presence, offering sacrifices as he goes, taking two goats, burning incense on the incense altar, eventually stepping past the dividing curtain into the most holy place, where he splashes blood onto a special piece of furniture.

In some English Bibles it gets translated as *mercy seat*, and this is yet *another* word we can thank Tyndale for. Again, there's no exact English equivalent, so Tyndale used Martin Luther's German translation—*gnadenstuhl. Gnadenstuhl* literally means "seat of grace," which is what Luther thought happened on this piece of furniture. Again, it's a pretty good word, but it can be so much richer once we recognise the Hebrew origins. The Hebrew word is a noun, *kapporeth*, and it's actually a noun form of the word *kippur*. And so if we understand *kippur* as wiping away, cleansing, purifying, then the *kapporeth* is the place of wiping away, or the cleansing object. This object sits on top of the ark of the covenant like a lid, which is why it sometimes gets translated as the purgation cover, the atonement lid, or the atoning cover. David calls it Yahweh's footstool (1 Chr 28:2), because it is on this cover that Yahweh's presence appears. And this is the bit that really blows me away: in the most holy place, where Yahweh's presence is most concentrated—*this* is the place where atonement is made, sin is dealt with, and relationship is restored. Not in a rubbish dump. Not outside the camp. Not in a courtroom. But in the middle of Yahweh's holy sanctuary, on his footstool called "atonement." Yahweh wants his dwelling place to be associated with atonement.

So here is high priest Aaron, standing in the most holy place, surrounded by a cloud of incense smoke, splashing blood onto Yahweh's footstool.

> Thus he shall make atonement for the Holy Place, be-
> cause of the uncleannesses of the people of Israel and

> because of their transgressions, all their sins. And so he shall do for the tent of meeting, which dwells with them in the midst of their uncleannesses. (Lev 16:16 ESV)

Part of the atoning ritual is to *wipe away* with blood all the sin that had piled up around Yahweh's tent over the course of the year, and then "when he has made an end of atoning for the Holy Place and the tent of meeting and the altar, he shall present the live goat" (16:20 ESV).

Once atonement has been made for the *space*, and it has been *wiped clean*, the second part of the drama unfolds with atonement being made for the *people*. After Aaron emerges from the most holy place, he takes the live goat, piles all Israel's iniquities, transgressions, and sins onto its head, and the whole unclean load of impurity, a year's worth of trash, is led away and dumped outside the camp, "and he shall let the goat go free in the wilderness" (v. 22 ESV). Then Aaron bathes his body, changes his clothes, offers a burnt offering and "make[s] atonement for himself and for the people" (v. 24).

At the end of the day, after this drama has been acted out, the space has been wiped clean, the tent and the Israelite camp has been restored to its former condition, and all the people have had their sin and impurity removed. Here's how Leviticus sums up Israel's condition at the end of the day: "You will be clean from all your sins before Yahweh" (v. 30).

A quick note on who this Azazel character might be, because it truly is scandalous. Many commentaries and scholars agree that Azazel must be a proper name, and this becomes apparent when noticing that one goat is "for Yahweh" and the other "for Azazel." I'm inclined to agree with the many commentators who claim that

Azazel is the proper name of a spirit, a goat demon, who haunts the desert. The Bible tells us that the Israelites believed there were demons lurking in the desert, including goat demons, and unfortunately they often felt the need to offer sacrifices to them (Isa 34:14, 2 Chr 11:15, Matt 12:43, Luke 8:29).

Do goat demons show up elsewhere in Jewish literature? You bet they do. The book of Enoch is a book you will find in your Bible if you are Ethiopian. The part of the book of Enoch that mentions Azazel dates to about 250 BC, and it is referenced in 2 Peter, while Jude straight up quotes from it. It contains an expanded retelling of the story of Gen 6, where Azazel is the leader of some kind of angelic rebellion who mingle with humans. In this story, Azazel gives knowledge of evil to humans, and is therefore seen to be worthy of having all sins ascribed to him. His punishment for defiling the whole earth is to be bound, sent to the wilderness, and placed in a pit.

> Bind Azâzêl hand and foot, and put him in the darkness; make an opening in the desert. . . . The whole earth was defiled through the example of the deeds of Azâzêl; to him ascribe all the Sins.[2]

This goat demon, who apparently deserves to have all sins attributed to him,[3] is therefore the worthy recipient of a goat carrying a year's worth of Israel's sin. It's not a sacrifice. It's not an offering. It's not a gift that anyone would want to be given. Not dissimilar to the Neo-Assyrian frog that returned evil to its steppe, Israel's sin is returned to its source: Azazel. It's more like a "return to sender." More like a "go back to where you came from."

Perhaps the book of Enoch and goat demons seems a bit far-fetched. Perhaps you're yelling at me, "Stay in your lane, Phil, stick to Leviticus." Well, you make a fair point. I hear your rebuke.

---

2. Schodde, *Book of Enoch*, 69.

3. If these ancient Jews conceived of one maleficent being who could defile the "whole earth," and who was somehow the source of "all sins," it was presumably already within Jewish conception that one merciful being could purify the "whole earth," and could remove "all sins" through his atoning work.

Back to Leviticus we go, and turn the page to chapter 17. Oh, wait, what's that in verse 7? A gosh darn goat demon!

The goat shall bear on itself all their iniquities to an uninhabited land; and he shall release the goat in the wilderness. (Lev 16:22 NKJV)

Previously I said that no other animal is said to bear sin. Well, that little word *bear* carries a lot of weight. In Hebrew the word is *nasa* and it means "carry," or "lift up." An easy way to remember it is to think about a NASA spaceship as "lifting off." This goat carries *nasa* iniquity, and iniquity is another Hebrew word we can learn: *avon*. Put them together and you have *nasa avon*—bear iniquity. We know what it looks like for the live goat to *nasa avon*, but what about a human? Several times in Leviticus we read a warning that if someone does wrong, they *nasa avon*: they bear their own iniquity, or their guilt remains on them.

If anyone sins . . . though he did not know it, then realizes his guilt, he shall bear his iniquity [*nasa avon*]. (5:17 ESV)

If he does not wash them or bathe his flesh, he shall [*nasa avon*] bear his iniquity. (17:16 ESV)

Everyone who eats it shall bear his iniquity [*nasa avon*]. (19:8 ESV)

It's an intriguing way to conceptualise wrongdoing. In English we say "please forgive me" or "I forgive you." But in Hebrew an offence is something that remains as a burden that the offender carries around. "If a person sins . . . he is guilty and shall bear his iniquity [*nasa avon*]" (Lev 5:17 NKJV). To experience forgiveness this person needs his burden of guilt or sin to be *lifted off* and removed. And this is what Leviticus is saying. Anyone who does wrong, or who doesn't repent and receive forgiveness, will continue to carry around the burden of their own iniquity. What they need is for someone to remove their burden.[4] *Nasa avon* is what the live goat did once a year; it carried away Israel's iniquity into the wilderness. But guess who else *nasa avon*?

> Yahweh is slow to anger and abundant in lovingkindness, [*nasa avon*] forgiving iniquity and transgression. (Num 14:18)

That's right, Yahweh bears iniquity. In this context it usually gets translated as *forgive*, but in Hebrew thought iniquity had weight. In an ancient mind, iniquity, sin, and impurity were real things with corrosive powers that caused real damage. They couldn't be waved away, or even swept under the carpet. They had to be dealt with. They had to be removed.

> I acknowledged my sin to you,
> and I did not cover my iniquity;
> I said, "I will confess my transgressions to the LORD,"
> and you [*nasa avon*] forgave the iniquity of my sin. (Ps 32:5 ESV)

In a sense, Yahweh gets his hands dirty; he picks up sin, he carries it, and he hurls it away with all his might.

> Who is a God like you, who [*nasa avon*] pardons sin and forgives the transgression of the remnant of his inheritance? You do not stay angry forever but delight to show mercy. You will again have compassion on us; you will tread our sins underfoot and hurl all our iniquities into the depths of the sea. (Mic 7:18–19 NIV)

And once a year Israel was privileged to watch God's character in action, acted out in a visceral visual drama. The live goat demonstrates what Yahweh does with sin: he removes it. He lifts it up and tosses it away, completing the cleansing act of atonement.

---

4. See Lam, *Patterns of Sin*. Joseph Lam has done extensive research on the various metaphors for sin found throughout the Hebrew Bible.

And at the end of the day, the Day of Atonement, a heavy layer of grime had been removed from the Israelite camp, "for it is on this day that atonement shall be made for you to cleanse you; you will be clean from all your sins before Yahweh" (Lev 16:30).

One day John was standing out in the wilderness, when suddenly he saw a man walking towards him. He exclaimed, "Behold, the Lamb of God, who takes away the sin of the world!" (John 1:29).

The man John was looking at was Jesus: Jesus, the lamb who takes away sin. We've met a sin-carrying goat, but have we met a lamb that removed sin? Perhaps the sin offering? But the sin offering was usually a bull. Occasionally a goat. Ah, wait, hidden right at the end of chapter 4: a female lamb can be offered. Does Jesus fit the category of female lamb? What about the Passover lamb? Definitely a lamb. Definitely male. But nowhere in the Passover story is there any mention of the word *sin*, much less this lamb taking away sin. Is this the appearance of the lamb of which Isaac queried, "Behold, the fire and the wood, but where is the lamb?" And Abraham responded, "God will provide for Himself the lamb" (Gen 22:7–8). Or perhaps John is referring to the silent lamb from Isa 53—but was this even a sacrificial lamb if it was being shorn (Isa 53:7)?

Regardless of the apparent lack of lambs that remove sin, Jesus does indeed take sin away: "He has appeared once for all at the end of the age to remove sin by the sacrifice of himself" (Heb 9:26 NRSV). And guess how he removed sin? Two verses later Hebrews reveals that Christ carried sin. "Christ, having been offered once to bear the sins of many" (Heb 9:28 NRSV).

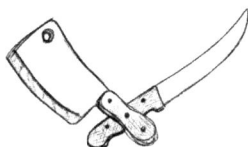

What is the best way to remove mould from your house? Vinegar? Bleach? Ammonia? Incorrect! The correct procedure is as follows:

> So he shall cleanse the house with the blood of the bird and with the running water, along with the live bird, the cedar wood, the hyssop, and the scarlet string. However, he shall let the live bird go free outside the city into the open field. So he shall make atonement for the house, and it will be clean. (Lev 14:52–53 NASB)

Technically this won't remove mould. This is to cleanse the house *after* a priest has established the mould has all gone. Here's the method: take two birds. Bird One is killed, and its blood is used to cleanse the house. Bird Two—the living bird—is sent away. Again, atonement is being made for an object—a house—with the blood from a clean animal being used as cleansing detergent. As the living bird is released, the dramatised message of atonement is communicated. What if we quickly revisit our friend from the chapter on slaughter, who thought that "the violent death of the animal signifies the penalty human beings deserve for their sin?"[5] We cannot possibly imagine that Bird One is receiving a violent vicarious punishment for a crime. Because buildings don't commit crimes. Buildings don't need a vicarious death. Neither is mould in a house a sin deserving death.

In Lev 14 there is another *two birds* ritual, but this time it's not a house being purified. This ritual describes the process for cleansing a person recovering from a skin disease. It involves two birds and a scarlet thread. Remember the ancient Hittite ritual where a red thread was tied to a mouse who was released? Or the

5. Schreiner, "Substitutionary Atonement," para. 7.

Neo-Assyrian Empire ritual where a red thread was tied to a frog who hopped away, carrying with it a disease? Here in the Hebrew version, Bird One is killed and its blood is collected. The second *live* bird is taken, along with the red thread, dipped in the blood and in running (clean) water, which is then sprinkled on the unclean person with the skin disease. The live bird is then sent out to fly away over an open field! The bird is released, carrying away the uncleanness, just like a goat taking away sin (or a frog or a mouse).

In both cases, the mouldy house or the person recovering from disease, if our focus is on the dead bird, we are focussing on the wrong place. These dramas point to life, cleansing, and removal of impurity. The lifeblood brings life and cleansing into a space that had been contaminated by death and impurity. And the live bird carries away the impurity and disease, leaving the space atoned for and cleansed. Atonement is not merely about wiping away sin, it's about removing disease too. Atonement is God's way of cleansing and restoring everything back to its original and intended condition.

Not many stories appear in all four Gospels, but when they do it's a sign to pay extra close attention. The story of Barabbas's release by Pilate is one such story, and the first clue to understanding its significance lies with the characters' names. Some early manuscripts tell us that this man's name was in fact Jesus Barabbas. The NIV reads, "a well-known prisoner whose name was Jesus Barabbas" (Matt 27:16).[6]

This scene reveals two men named Jesus. Both playing the role of a saviour figure. Both trying to personify the meaning of

6. The NIV includes the footnote that "many manuscripts do not have Jesus" (Matt 27:16).

the name Jesus which means "Yahweh saves." Both trying to rescue people from Roman occupation, but going about it in completely different ways—one Jesus by committing violence and killing, the other Jesus by allowing himself to be violently killed.

The parallels become more apparent when we discover what Barabbas means. The Greek name Barabbas comes from the Aramaic *Bar Abba* which means "son of the father." So we are presented with two prisoners. Both with a name meaning *Yahweh saves*. One named "Jesus son of the father." One named "Jesus son of God." Both on trial. Almost identical, wouldn't you say? Almost like two identical goats? Especially when we note that one is guilty and one is blameless. And especially when we notice that Pilate plans to *release* one of them. "Whom do you want me to release for you? Barabbas, or Jesus who is called Christ?" (Matt 27:17).

In Leviticus the choice of which goat to release was given to Yahweh, through the casting of lots by a priest. But in this story the religious leaders invite the people to decide, and appallingly they make the wrong choice. Rather than releasing the innocent Jesus, they demand the release of the guilty. And in a devastating twist, Matthew points out that "all the people replied, 'His blood shall be on us and on our children!'" (Matt 27:25 NASB). They were calling for Jesus' blood because they wanted him crucified. But Matthew words it in this harrowingly ironic way to show that what they intended for evil, God intended for good. Jesus' blood would indeed be on them, but, mercifully, to purify them and their children from their sin. Although the people called for the wrong one to be released, the one who was wrongly condemned is the one who would release them from their wrongs.

Removing sin is only half the drama, however. The Day of Atonement contains another scene: the cleansing act. Performing this drama, high priest Aaron takes "the goat of the sin offering, which is for the people" (Lev 16:15 NASB), slaughters it, then carrying the blood he steps past the curtain and into the most holy place, where he sprinkles the blood on the atoning cover, and makes atonement for all the people of Israel.

But apparently, according to Hebrews, "it is impossible for the blood of bulls and goats to take away sins" (Heb 10:4 NASB). And besides, high priest Aaron will have to repeat the drama again the next year. And every year after that. And then he will die.

Today, however, we have a better high priest. We have a high priest who lives forever (Heb 7:24). A high priest who always lives to make intercession for us (v. 25). A high priest who is holy and blameless and unstained by sin (v. 26). "Unlike the other high priests, he does not need to offer sacrifices day after day, first for his own sins, and then for the sins of the people. He sacrificed for their sins once for all when he offered himself" (v. 27 NIV). And then he sat down at the right hand of God (10:12). And so, since we have Jesus as our high priest, interceding for us forever, and because of Jesus' own purifying blood, we too can enter the most holy place, and draw near to God.

> Therefore, brothers and sisters, since we have confidence to enter the Most Holy Place by the blood of Jesus, by a new and living way opened for us through the curtain, that is, his body, and since we have a great priest over the house of God, let us draw near to God. (Heb 10:19–22 NIV)

Atonement is bigger than a single symbol of blood, or isolated action of wiping. Atonement is God's big picture way of pointing to the day when death and disease and defilement will all be wiped away, in a recreated Eden space. And this is where Tyndale's made-up word makes most sense, because atonement is about God and humanity dwelling together in a restored relationship. No more sin. No more disease. No more death.

And what better picture is there of God's character than a goat, laden with a big burden of sin, carrying away all iniquity? The image of the goat being led away gave the Israelites a yearly reminder of what God does to sin. He removes it. As I think of Yahweh removing sin I'm reminded of the beautiful words of David in Ps 103.

> He does not deal with us according to our sins,
> nor repay us according to our iniquities [*avon*].
> For as high as the heavens are above the earth,
> so great is his steadfast love toward those who fear him;
> as far as the east is from the west,
> so far does he remove our transgressions from us.
> (Ps 103:10–12 ESV)

Just now as I write this, I notice that those same three words used for sin appear here together. Surely David must have been meditating on the Day of Atonement as he wrote this psalm. I can imagine David standing forlornly, hearing all his sins and failures being heaped on top of this goat. He watches as the man leads this goat, labouring under its heavy burden, and they slowly disappear into the distance. He watches the goat getting smaller and smaller as it is led further and further away until finally they're lost from sight and his sin is gone. He takes a long, deep breath. He feels a little bit lighter. Like a weight that he had been carrying all year has been lifted off.

> As the east is far from the west,
> He has distanced from us our transgressions.[7]

7. Ps 103:12, Alter, *Hebrew Bible*, 240.

Sunday morning. Silence. An intrusive cough echoes around the bare brick walls. A tray appears before my bowed head. I pick up a lifeless square of sliced, white, store-bought bread. Silence. No bleating goats. No bellowing bulls. I long for a crackling fire, but there is no roasting meat, no kidneys, no liver, no fatty portions hissing and sputtering. I take a deep breath. There is no pleasing aroma. This space doesn't smell uniquely sacred. Actually, it smells just like the local cafe I visit every morning. Absent is any incense or frankincense. I look up. There is no fragrant smoke ascending. I look around. Four bare walls. No art. No helpful imagery. No symbolism. The space feels sterile, but not because it has been cleansed with blood. Another tray appears, full of plastic disposable cups of grape juice. I take one. The grave silence persists. I am surrounded by people I love, my friends, my family, yet I feel isolated. We are sharing a meal, yet this meal is unlike any other meal. We are about to eat together but we won't talk. We will drink together but we won't look at each other. This meal is unlike any other meal. The square of bread squashed between my thumb and forefinger is supposed to be Jesus' unblemished body, but it doesn't feel like fatty portions; it doesn't even feel like particularly good bread. As I struggle to appreciate the unimaginable depth, and weight, and glory of Jesus' life, the plastic cup feels flimsy and weightless in my hand.

Yet Jesus' blood is life. Can a cup contain the Creator of the universe? Can a cup hold the life-blood of the Creator of all life?

This meal is unlike any other meal. Should we not shout? Can we not celebrate? Is this not the greatest feast ever? Surely there is more significance in this meal than in all sacrifices ever offered; more sustenance in this food than in a thousand grain offerings; more weight in this piece of bread than in any sermon ever preached—because the Word became flesh, and, as this bread enters our mouths and fills our bodies, we are consuming the Word of God himself. The one who sustains life has given us bread to sustain our souls.[8]

8. "The bread which God the Word revealed to be his own body is the Word of the sustainer of souls. What was set upon the table was the Word proceeding

The silence is shattered as the priest recites Jesus' words.

> This is My body which is given for you; do this in re-
> membrance of Me. (Luke 22:19 NKJV)

When Jesus uttered those words, he was very much alive, sharing a meal, the Passover sacrifice, with his best friends. This meal is unlike any other meal. When we eat this meal, we can and should reflect on his death, as Paul says (1 Cor 11:26). But we remember more than just Jesus' death, we remember Jesus himself! "Do this in remembrance of Me," says Jesus. His actions. His selflessness. His compassion. His mercy. His life. To paraphrase Jesus' own words: if you eat my body, you have life in you (John 6:53).

And as we eat, we are not merely remembering an historical event, we are not impassive spectators on the sideline,[9] we are

---

from God the Word, bread from heavenly bread." Archdiocese for the Military Services, USA, "Eucharistic Reflections" (quoting Origen's *Commentary on Matthew*).

9. "They were not only spectators of the drama (watching and listening) but participants in it (eating and drinking). Just so today the Lord's Supper is more than a 'commemoration', by which we recall an event of the past; it is a

part of the story, we are participants in the event. As we partake of Jesus' body and blood, Jesus himself is present, and together we are participating in his *once for all* sacrifice.

Again, the priest proclaims Jesus' words:

> He took the cup, gave thanks, and gave to them, saying, "All of you drink it, for this is my blood of the new covenant, which is poured out for many for the remission of sins." (Matt 26:27–28 HNV[10])

The purifying life-blood of Jesus is given for us and to us, injecting life into bodies that have been infected with a death disease. For the remission[11] and removal of sins, "the blood of Jesus Christ His Son cleanses us from all sin" (1 John 1:7 NKJV).

Every goat, every unblemished lamb, the tent, the priesthood, every drop of sprinkled blood, all were shadows cast by a glorious reality. But now we behold the shape casting the shadows, the person of Jesus. Now we look up from shadows on the ground, and we recognise the radiant reality, the glorious Substance whose presence pervades all things with his eternal light.

We are not eating shadows, we are feasting on the Substance. We are not drawing near to a shadowy tent, we are drawing near to God himself. We are not presenting shadowy food on a shadowy altar, we are seated at the Lord's heavenly table, in the glorious presence of Christ himself.

> The flesh feeds on the body and blood of Christ, that the soul likewise may be filled with God.[12]

'communion', by which we share in its present benefits." Stott, "Lord's Supper."

10. The Hebrew Names Version (HNV) is based off the World English Bible, an update of the American Standard Version of 1901. This version of the Bible is in the public domain.

11. Often translated as *forgiveness*, the Greek word can mean *send away* or *release*. It's the same word Jesus reads from the Isaiah scroll when he proclaims "*release* to the captives" (John 4:18), and is related to the Greek word we explored in the "Bonus Chapter," when Jesus says "Your sins are forgiven" (Luke 5:20, 7:48).

12. Tertullian, "Resurrection of the Flesh," chap. 8.

Bibliography

Adamson, Andrew, and Vicky Jenson, dirs. *Shrek*. Redwood City, CA: PDI/ DreamWorks Pictures, 2001.

Alter, Robert. *The Hebrew Bible: A Translation with Commentary*. New York: Norton, 2019.

Archdiocese for the Military Services, USA. "Eucharistic Reflections, Lectio Divina: Origen of Alexandria, Priest." Archdiocese for the Military Services, USA. https://files.milarch.org/offices/evangelization/lectio-divina/lectio-divina-origen.pdf.

Aristeas. "The Letter of Aristeas." Edited by R. H. Charles. Oxford: Clarendon, 1913. Revised by Joshua Williams. Christian Classics Ethereal Library, 1995. https://www.ccel.org/c/charles/otpseudepig/aristeas.htm.

Athanasius. *On the Incarnation*. Translated by Penelope Lawson. Monergism. https://www.monergism.com/thethreshold/sdg/athanasius/On%20the%20Incarnation%20-%20Athanasius.pdf.

Ayali-Darshan, Noga. "The Scapegoat Ritual and Its Ancient Near Eastern Parallels." TheTorah.com, 2020. www.thetorah.com/article/the-scapegoat-ritual-and-its-ancient-near-eastern-parallels.

Britannica Dictionary. "Sacrifice." *Encyclopaedia Britannica*. https://www.britannica.com/dictionary/sacrifice.

Davis, Jeremy. *Welcoming Gifts: Sacrifice in the Bible and Christian Life*. Munster, IN: Ancient Faith, 2022.

Douglas, Mary. *Leviticus as Literature*. Oxford: Oxford University Press, 1999.

Guthrie, Nancy. "The Provision of Sacrifice in the Old Testament." Crossway, May 26, 2019. www.crossway.org/articles/the-provision-of-sacrifice-in-the-old-testament.

Kaplan, Abby. *Misreading Ritual: Sacrifice and Purity for the Modern-Day Gentile*. Eugene, OR: Resource, 2022. Ebook.

Lam, Joseph. *Patterns of Sin in the Hebrew Bible: Metaphor, Culture, and the Making of a Religious Concept*. Oxford: Oxford University Press, 2016.

Mackie, Tim. "Glory." *BibleProject*. Podcast. The Language of Faith series, episode 2. Oct. 17, 2017.

Milgrom, Jacob. *Leviticus: A Book of Ritual and Ethics*. Minneapolis: Fortress, 2004.

Morales, L. Michael. *Who Shall Ascend the Mountain of the Lord? A Biblical Theology of the Book of Leviticus*. Downers Grove, IL: InterVarsity, 2015.

Nagasawa, Mako A. *Christmas with Irenaeus: How Jesus' Incarnation Honors Creation, Human Body, and the Human Story*. Dublin: Trinity, 2023.

Philo. "The Works of Philo: The Special Laws, I." Translated by C. D. Yonge. Early Christian Writings. https://www.earlychristianwritings.com/yonge/book27.html.

Rillera, Andrew Remington. *Lamb of the Free: Recovering the Varied Sacrificial Understandings of Jesus's Death*. Eugene, OR: Cascade, 2024.

Schodde, George H., trans. and ed. *The Book of Enoch: Translated from the Ethiopic with Introduction and Notes*. Andover, MA: Draper, 1911.

Schreiner, Thomas. "Substitutionary Atonement." Gospel Coalition. https://www.thegospelcoalition.org/essay/substitutionary-atonement.

Stott, John. "The Lord's Supper." Sydney Anglicans, Oct. 12, 2004. https://sydneyanglicans.net/news/the_lords_supper.

Tertullian. "On the Resurrection of the Flesh." In *Ante-Nicene Fathers*. Vol. 3. Translated by Peter Holmes. Edited by Alexander Roberts et al. Buffalo, NY: Christian Literature, 1885. Revised and edited by Kevin Knight. New Advent. https://www.newadvent.org/fathers/0316.htm.

Thiessen, Matthew. *Jesus and the Forces of Death: The Gospels' Portrayal of Ritual Impurity Within First-Century Judaism*. Grand Rapids: Baker Academic, 2021.

Walton, John H. *Ancient Near Eastern Thought and the Old Testament*. Grand Rapids: Baker Academic, 2006.

Whitaker, Maja I. *Perfect in Weakness: Disability and Human Flourishing in the New Creation*. Waco, TX: Baylor University Press, 2023.